America Under Attack:
Primary
Sources

Other titles in the Lucent Terrorism Library are:

America Under Attack: September 11, 2001
The History of Terrorism
Terrorists and Terrorist Groups

THE
LUCENT
TERRORISM
LIBRARY

America Under Attack:
Primary Sources

Tamara L. Roleff, Editor

LUCENT BOOKS
SAN DIEGO, CALIFORNIA

THOMSON
————✶————™
GALE

Detroit • New York • San Diego • San Francisco
Boston • New Haven, Conn. • Waterville, Maine
London • Munich

Library of Congress Cataloging-in-Publication Data

America Under Attack : Primary Sources / Tamara L. Roleff, book editor.
        p. cm. — (Lucent terrorism library)
Summary: Looks at the September 11, 2001, terrorist attack on the World Trade Center and Pentagon
U.S. response, world reaction, and the war on terrorism.
Includes bibliographical references and index.
        ISBN 1-59018-216-2 (hardback : alk. paper)
    1. September 11 Terrorist Attacks, 2001—Juvenile literature. 2. War on Terrorism, 2001—Juvenile
literature. 3. Terrorism—United States—Juvenile literature. [1. September 11 Terrorist Attacks, 2001.
2. War on Terrorism, 2001– 3. Terrorism.] I. Roleff, Tamara L., 1959– II. Terrorism library series.
    HV6432 .A52 2002
    973.931—dc21

2002001816

Contents

Foreword

It was the bloodiest day in American history since the battle of Antietam during the Civil War—a day in which everything about the nation would change forever. People, when speaking of the country, would henceforth specify "before September 11" or "after September 11." It was as if, on that Tuesday morning, the borders had suddenly shifted to include Canada and Mexico, or as if the official language of the United States had changed. The difference between "before" and "after" was that pronounced.

That Tuesday morning, September 11, 2001, was the day that Americans began to learn firsthand about terrorism, as first one fuel-heavy commercial airliner, and then a second, hit New York's World Trade Towers—sending them thundering to the ground in a firestorm of smoke and ash. A third airliner was flown into a wall of the Pentagon in Washington, D.C., and a fourth was apparently wrestled away from terrorists before it could be steered into another building. By the time the explosions and collapses had stopped and the fires had been extinguished, more than three thousand Americans had died.

Film clips and photographs showed the horror of that day. Trade Center workers could be seen leaping to their deaths from seventy, eighty, ninety floors up rather than endure the 1,000-degree temperatures within the towers. New Yorkers who had thought they were going to work, were caught on film desperately racing the other way to escape the wall of dust and debris that rolled down the streets of lower Manhattan. Photographs showed badly burned Pentagon secretaries and frustrated rescue workers. Later pictures would show huge fire engines buried under the rubble.

It was not the first time America had been the target of terrorists. The same World Trade Center had been targeted in 1993 by Islamic terrorists, but the results had been negligible. The worst of such acts on American soil came in 1995 at the hands of a home-grown terrorist whose hatred for the government led to the bombing of the federal building in Oklahoma City. The blast killed 168 people—19 of them children.

But the September 11 attacks were far different. It was terror on a frighteningly well-planned, larger scale, carried out by nineteen men from the Middle East whose hatred of the United States drove them to the most appalling suicide mission the world had ever witnessed. As one U.S. intelligence officer told a CNN reporter, "These guys turned airplanes into weapons of mass destruction, landmarks familiar to all of us into mass graves."

Some observers say that September 11 may always be remembered as the date that the people of the United States finally came face to face with terrorism. "You've been relatively sheltered from terrorism," says an Israeli terrorism expert. "You hear about it happening here in the Middle East, in Northern Ireland, places far away from you. Now Americans have joined the real world where this ugliness is almost a daily occurrence."

This "real world" presents a formidable challenge to the United States and other nations. It is a world in which there are no rules, where modern terrorism is war not waged on soldiers, but on innocent people— including children. Terrorism is meant to shatter people's hope, to create instability in their daily lives, to make them feel vulnerable and frightened. People who continue to feel unsafe will demand that their leaders make concessions—do *something*—so that terrorists will stop the attacks.

Many experts feel that terrorism against the United States is just beginning. "The tragedy is that other groups, having seen [the success of the September 11 attacks] will think: why not do something else?" says Richard Murphy, former ambassador to Syria and Saudi Arabia. "This is the beginning of their war. There is a mentality at work here that the West is not prepared to understand."

Because terrorism is abhorrent to the vast majority of the nations on the planet, President George W. Bush's declaration of war against terrorism was supported by many other world leaders. He reminded citizens that it would be a long war, and one not easily won. However, as many agree, there is no choice; if terrorism is allowed to continue unchecked the world will never be safe.

The four volumes of the Lucent Terrorism Library help to explain the unexplainable events of September 11, 2001, as well as examine the history and personalities connected with terrorism in the United States and elsewhere in the world. Annotated bibliographies provide readers with ideas for further research. Fully documented primary and secondary source quotations enliven the text. Each book in this series provides students with a wealth of information as well as launching points for further study and discussion.

Chapter One

On the Scene

As New York City's morning news shows were winding up their broadcasts on Tuesday, September 11, 2001, reports began trickling in that an airplane had crashed into the North Tower (Tower 1) of the World Trade Center in Manhattan. Footage of the burning tower appeared live on televisions across the United States. Many people initially thought that a small, personal airplane had crashed into the building. This belief changed about twenty minutes later when a second airplane—a Boeing 767—flew straight into the second tower (the South Tower) of the World Trade Center. Suddenly it became clear that the crashes were not accidents; the planes had been hijacked and flown deliberately into the buildings.

By the time the second plain hit, almost every television station and radio channel in the world provided live coverage of the attacks. People watched and listened as the twin towers burned. Firefighters rushed to the scene, and paramedics loaded supplies onto ambulances as frightened office workers fled the area. Then, about an hour after the attack began, the South Tower collapsed, its structural support beams melting from the heat of the fire. The North Tower soon followed, leaving the area covered in rubble and ash. By the time it was over, around 3,000 people had died.

Meanwhile, networks reported that two other planes had also crashed—one into the Pentagon in Washington, D.C., killing 189 people, and one into a field southeast of Pittsburgh, Pennsylvania, killing all forty-five passengers and crew on board. As these reports came in, many people began to believe the four crashes were an attack against the United States. In response, politicians and military leaders called the attacks an act of war and vowed that they would not go unpunished.

Escape from the Seventy-Second Floor

Mehdi Dadgarian is a civil engineer from Ann Arbor, Michigan, who also works as a consultant to the New York City Port Authority. He had arrived in New York City on September 10, 2001, for a meeting at the World Trade Center the following day. He was making telephone calls in his office on the seventy-second floor of the World Trade Center's North Tower when the first plane crashed into the building. Below is his account of his escape from the tower.

How can I not believe in miracles when I walked out of the World Trade Center unhurt? How can I not believe in love when I see the outpouring of it from the friends and family who have been calling and e-mailing me since the attack? Rather than seeing the world as an uglier place after the attack, I see it as a beautiful place where people give all they can when called upon to do so.

I will never forget the police and firemen who walked past me to save lives in the building and never walked out. Those who went in knowing that the chances were good they would never walk out. I will never forget the people I worked with who were not as lucky as me. As the stories come out about those who did not make it, you realize how every second made such a difference; how one wrong decision could have been fatal.

When I visited New York, I usually worked on the 72nd floor of the North Tower (Tower 1). I had arrived in the city late on Monday night, September 10th. The next day a group of us from Bechtel and the Port

Authority were going to attend Primavera's user conference in Philadelphia.

Going up the North Tower elevator I decided to spend some time responding to e-mails and then get ready by 10 A.M. when we were supposed to leave for Philadelphia. At 8:40 A.M. I remember I was on the phone leaving a message for one of the Port Authority division managers when the first plane hit our tower (North Tower) at about the 90th floor, I even remember saying "Oh my God we got hit . . . Oh my God we got hit!" in my phone message.

When the plane hit, it was nowhere near as dramatic as you would think on the 72nd floor, compared to the higher floors. There was a loud explosion and the building shook violently. There was a big flash of light. The really scary part was how much the building moved, and kept moving, for a long time before stabilizing. At the same time we saw out the window that flaming pieces of the building were flying past our floor window on their way down.

People on our floor were a little confused, not knowing to stay or evacuate. I heard some of the secretaries crying and hugging each other. The floor wardens with their red hats had not yet mobilized to give us instructions. They probably would have suggested we stay in the hall and wait for an announcement.

Not knowing what hit us, I didn't feel it was anything serious, so I went back to my desk to finish answering my e-mails. Next I noticed the smoke filling the floor and most of the people had already evacuated the floor. One of the Port Authority managers asked me what I was doing there and that I needed to leave immediately. I asked him if everybody had been evacuated. He told me he wasn't sure and if I wanted I could search the floor. So I started running on the floor and shouting... "Everybody has to evacuate immediately!" By then it was only me and the manager left on the floor.

We moved toward the stairs to leave when we heard cries from the elevator. Four people were stuck in it. We tried to open the elevator door, but to no avail. I ran back to the office trying to find some tool to use as a lever. I found a heavy-duty stapler that we tried to use to pry the elevator door open. We tried for ten minutes and we could only open the door a few inches leaving the stapler between the doors so they could get some air, even though there was smoke in the air, but still it was better than the air in the elevator.

By now the floor was getting really hot and full of smoke, our eyes were burning. I was running back and forth to the men's room and bringing wet paper towel to put on our eyes and the eyes of the people in the elevator. By now my survival instincts were kicking in and I knew that we needed to leave. So I told my comrade in arm that we need to leave since we could not do anything for the people in the elevator except to let the firemen know. He told me I should leave since I have young kids. He was going to stay so he could tell the firemen about the people in the elevator.

I started my descent with my heart still with the people on the 72nd floor. The stairs were deserted. I started to get worried and thought I had stayed too long, not knowing the full danger of the moment. I was able to

get to the 40th floor fairly easily. After that we were slowed up by people coming in from other floors. Some were crying, some were tired and not in good shape, but we all helped the weaker ones.

There were several times when two landings ahead of me were empty because I was helping a heavy woman named Michelle. She was having trouble with her knees. No one pushed past, no one yelled at us. Many had been in the last World Trade Center bombing in 1993, and they kept telling us what we were going through was much better than that time. The lights were on, the smoke was not so bad, the fire was on the floors above. We were going to make it out.

It wasn't until all the flow of traffic on the stairs stopped that people got panicky and started to yell. But then a stop-and-go pattern developed and we were calm again. I started to worry about my wife and kids. I wasn't ready to die yet. We started to hear that a plane had hit the building, and I wondered if it might not bounce into the other tower. I kept trying to dial my cell phone but it wouldn't work. No surprise.

We kept walking down the stairs. The smoke was getting thick. For a brief moment I thought we may get poisoned, that perhaps we were not yet safe. But that passed quickly too. Of course we were safe, we were near the ground (just 20 or so flights to go). We saw the first rescue worker coming up our stairway on the 17th floor. It slowed us down a little more, but we had all the time in the world, or so we thought.

When we were almost all the way down we came upon a floor that had water pouring out from under the door. This caused a waterfall the rest of the way down. There were several inches of water on the floor, but it was passable and did not slow us up much. We came out on the mezzanine level to the street level in the front of the building. It had taken us about 50 minutes to get down the stairs. There was probably less than a few minutes before the South Tower would collapse.

The plaza was filled with burning debris, but it did not look very bad—that is until you looked again. The sight of a heart stuck in its

A stairwell offers one of the few routes of escape before the Twin Towers collapse.

entirety against the mezzanine window got my attention. So I looked again at the plaza debris and all of a sudden I noticed a horrible scene of body parts and human organs, maimed bodies all over the plaza. Arms, legs, guts, half bodies, a site that I would never ever forget as long as I live. I kept thinking this can't be real, it's a movie. Oh how much I wanted it to be just that.

The lower level windows to West Street were completely blown out, but nothing looked bad out in the street. It was then; however, that the seriousness of the situation became apparent. The police had panic in their voice. They yelled at us with a real sense of urgency to move. When we came out of the stairwell the police asked us to walk in single file and do not run. After we got to the concourse level they were asking us to run. You very quickly realized you were not safe yet.

At the lower level they routed us through the basement mall. It was a surreal scene. It was completely empty except for a few rescue workers, the lights were out, the sprinklers were all going off and the floor was flooded. We ran down the corridor past the PATH [commuter] train, I saw the doors on the north side of the tower and the street there looked fine, but they were making us go a different way. That door was closer, but I decided to trust the police so I went up the escalator and out the door by the Borders bookstore at the northeast corner of the complex.

When we got outside they yelled for us to run, some stuff was on the ground and I realized that I could still be killed by falling debris. They kept yelling, "Don't look up!"

but I couldn't help myself. I turned around to see the fate of the buildings. Both towers had been hit. I kind of froze looking up at the magnificent towers with fire and smoke bellowing out of them.

I still did not feel safe right at the base of the buildings where many had stopped to watch people throwing themselves from the building. I saw the looks of horror on the onlookers' faces and I knew I did not want to look back. I saw one policeman scream that

The second of the two towers crumbles, spraying debris over the people and streets below.

another body was falling and then quickly turn his head away. There was nothing I wanted to see back in that building. Those were not images I could bear to imprint on my memory cells so they could haunt me for decades to come.

I moved fast, searching only for a free phone to call my wife and kids (my wife is in California and my kids are in upstate New York). At this time more debris started to fall from the South Tower along with loud crackling sounds. Somehow I knew that something bad was going to happen and I started to run for my life. That's when the South Tower started to fall.

I had somehow injured my left knee coming down the stairs and I couldn't run fast, but it was a matter of life and death. I wasn't going to let anything happen to me as long as I could help it. I was able to outrun the falling building but not the thick smoke. I remember running and kept looking back and seeing the smoke getting closer and closer until finally it engulfed us and turned the sunshine into darkness and horror. People began screaming and others in the street ran by the building (think of Godzilla movies).

The South Tower was the second to be hit and the first to fall. It had collapsed, imploding upon itself. Later I learned that the smoke was traveling at 50 miles an hour covering a two-mile radius. After the smoke got clear I found myself covered in what seemed like gray ash. Medics had set up a makeshift station to tend to the injured. I had difficulty breathing so I was given some oxygen and a mask and kept there for what seemed like an eternity.

Thinking back to that moment I do not remember hearing the sound of the building falling, the sound that people said was like a bomb exploding. All I remember was running away from smoke and then darkness and silence.

 ## The Towers Were Gone!

Barton Gellman, a newspaper correspondent who has covered terrorism in Jerusalem and other parts of the Middle East, was working as a reporter for the Washington Post *in New York City on September 11, 2001. He was unaware of the attacks against the World Trade Center just a few miles away from his office until his editor in Washington, D.C., called him. Gellman turned on his television in time to see the second plane fly into the South Tower. In the following story for the* American Journalism Review, *Gellman writes that he could not believe his eyes when the familiar Twin Towers were no longer a part of the city's skyline.*

It was one of those incongruous calls of the satellite age: Distant editor rings local scribe to say, in effect, look out your window. My window is miles uptown and points the wrong way, but I tuned the television in time to see a jetliner pierce the skin of the World Trade Center's south tower. In that first telescopic picture, before the dramatic closeups to come, the aircraft looked small, almost insubstantial, against the facade.

The next few steps came by rote. I had been a correspondent in the Middle East through seven suicide bombings and many smaller attacks. Boots, jeans, cash. No notebook, damn. All right—index cards. Just before walking out: binoculars and flashlight. On the street, no taxi wanted to go downtown. The subway seemed too big a risk. What if it got stuck? Never trust your mobility to a contraption that can imprison you for hours. I used the old New York standby of waving a bunch of $20 bills at an unlicensed limousine and took the FDR Drive south as far as the driver would go. When he refused to weave into the side streets around City Hall, I started walking. A Harley-Davidson came motoring along, its huge bearded rider wearing a disposable yellow camera like a bauble. He let me link hands around his substantial midsection, and we snaked through streets that were starting to fill with smoke.

When Harley Man began coughing, he stopped the bike and wished me luck. I walked on, doubling back when the streets were too thick with smoke and soot and circling to blocks that looked clearer. One short block, where the fire must have blazed but could not be seen, was so black at 10 A.M. that I actually used the Maglite to find my retreat.

It was an otherworldly landscape, heaped with drifts of ash and dust and papers by the tens of millions, smoldering and burning in piles. I pulled the T-shirt over my nose and mouth and cursed my failure to bring so much as a bandana. A guy in Haz-Mat gear looked at me sharply and told me I should know better than to walk toward the site; a police officer, disgusted at the proffer [offer]

A firefighter leads two people to safety after airliners slam into the World Trade Center's twin towers.

of a press card, offered to put me in the hospital if I did not turn around. In his heart-pounding zeal, I think he meant well.

I walked north for half a block and then cut west and doubled back. I could not quite get oriented: There was the north tower burning—the one with the television mast—but where was its twin? Was it the angle, or some obstruction? Unhappily I had no radio, something I never forgot when traveling overseas. Mobile circuits were jammed, of course, and my phone had accumulated so much dust that I thought I had better keep it covered anyway.

A few blocks north and east of the tower, I stopped next to a woman weeping as she goggled at the blazing gash in the tower's skin. And then everything got all mixed up in an almighty blow to the senses: a huge, low, rumbling, almost subsonic wave that resonated inside our bodies and filled our ears and seemed to go on a long time. I have felt only one thing at all like it before, while standing on a carrier flight deck for the launch of an F-14.

At the same time the smoky blaze of the tower became a boiling black cloud. And when the cloud began to clear a few seconds later, the tower was simply not there. GONE!! I wrote stupidly on an index card, underlining it three times. I could think of nothing else to write. In my shock I became aware that the woman next to me was screaming: "Oh, God, Oh, God, my niece works in that building! Oh, God." And as I recovered enough to help her sit down and to ask her name and the name of her niece, the next wave of the catastrophe arrived.

Two billion pounds of rubble were crashing down in the open esplanade around the World Trade Center, and the seething mass of ash and pulverized concrete struck the bottlenecks of lower Manhattan's adjacent canyons. Pressing outward and upward, the cloud rolled toward us, and we had to run. Stopping at Foley Square, outside the courthouse you see on "Law & Order," I watched survivors stumble in. They had been much closer than I, and ashes filled their throats and ears and noses. They were ash people, undistinguishable by hair color or

clothing. They plunged their heads and shoulders into the black marble fountain, retching. It felt like the end of the world we knew, and maybe the feeling was right.

Excerpted from "The Cloud Rolled Toward Us, and We Had to Run," by Barton Gellman, *American Journalism Review,* October 2001. Copyright © 2001 by *American Journalism Review.* Reprinted with permission.

 ## Waiting for Patients

When emergency services were notified of the plane crashes at the World Trade Center, firefighters, police officers, and medical personnel rushed immediately to the towers to help in any way they could. Matthew Klam, a contributing writer for the New York Times, *volunteered to help doctors and nurses care for the wounded. He describes the frustration they felt as they waited in vain for injured victims to appear.*

We needed bodies. Without them, we were useless. And so we kept waiting, staring south toward the billowing smoke, anxiously tapping our feet, hoping the ambulances constantly pulling up with their sirens blaring had somebody inside we could help. They didn't.

We sat where a mobile hospital was being thrown together in the courtyard of the Salomon Smith Barney building at 388 Greenwich. We were set up in teams. Each of us had tape across our shirts identifying our names and any special qualifications, like "skilled electrician."

It was early afternoon on the day of the blast. I'd gotten past the police barricades by sticking close to my new friend, Mark, whom I met on 42nd and Sixth that morning. Mark is a former critical-care nurse who retired four years ago. I saw him standing in the street, berating a cop for not knowing how to ferry qualified caregivers like him to the scene. I told Mark I wanted to help too; when he flagged down a uniformed fireman in a blue Corolla, I got in back.

Downtown, Mark took charge immediately. He volunteered to oversee pediatric and adult critical triage. He explained to me that our makeshift hospital would be a "stabilization platform." Badly injured people would be brought here to be stabilized, then transferred to area hospitals.

Fighting exhaustion, two firefighters continue the search for survivors in the rubble of the collapsed World Trade Center towers.

That was the plan. But we had only two patients: two guys in business attire breathing from oxygen masks, nurses hovering above them. They soon got up and left.

In their wake, a TV crew from "20/20" arrived. Matthew Modine, the actor, arrived in jeans and T-shirt and a baseball hat, also looking for some way to volunteer. It was my weirdest celebrity sighting ever.

With alarm, Mark told me that we only had 10 or so IV bags, not enough stethoscopes, very few hypos or epinephrine. "People are going to come here and die because we don't have this stuff," he said angrily.

Yeah. It was horrible. Except we didn't have any people dying or ailing. After two hours, the greatest difficulty was too many volunteers. People began endless discussions about where, exactly, to stack body boards. Meanwhile, more ambulances pulled up with roaring sirens; each time, nobody was in the back.

Excerpted from "Waiting," by Matthew Klam, *New York Times Magazine*, September 23, 2001. Copyright © 2001 by Matthew Klam. Reprinted with permission.

Searching for Survivors at the Pentagon

Members of the armed forces at the Pentagon in Washington, D.C., were watching live television coverage of the plane crashes into the World Trade Center towers when another hijacked plane hit the Pentagon. Colonel Robert J. Jenkins, a chaplain stationed in Korea, was attending a meeting at the Pentagon on September 11 when the plane hit the building. In the following account taken from his journal, Jenkins describes how survivors tried to rescue those who were trapped in the building, but that they were forced to abandon their attempts due to the heat and smoke.

September 11, 2001, day one. All Command Chaplains serving Commander In Chiefs (CINCS) from around the world (ten of us) had just concluded morning devotions in the Office of the Secretary of Defense (OSD) conference room in the Pentagon, had been given an overview for the week's annual Strategic Planning Conference conducted by the Joint Staff Chaplain and were on a ten-minute break when we were all called immediately back together to pray for the victims of the Trade Center attack now flashing on the briefing screen. Right after that prayer I was on the phone returning a call to my deputy command chaplain in Korea when I heard a very deep "boom."

Immediately everyone was exiting the conference room and franticly waving at me to follow. I hung up the phone and followed the orderly mass of people exiting the building. As we turned around we could see dark billowing rolls of smoke rising directly opposite from where we were. No one was panicking. No one was running. All of us were stunned in disbelief. We moved to the edge of the walkway and watched the smoke rise. Some were asking if it was a bomb. No one knew.

Word quickly passed through us that a plane had crashed into the other side of the building. The smoke was worse now. Suddenly security personnel began yelling at us to move off of the walkway and across the road to the river. Another plane was supposedly inbound for a second strike. No one seemed to panic, but anxiety obviously rose as folks now very quickly moved down the steps and across the road. I lost sight of my master sergeant, but I knew she got out ahead of me. In utter disbelief, I too moved to the road. An F-16 suddenly screamed by overhead and caused everyone to duck. Some uttered words that probably reflected what many others were at least thinking. A policeman said the aircraft had been identified as friendly. We were relieved.

Casualties began emerging toward us from inside the building. Some were walking on their own while others were being helped or carried. Voices were calling for anyone with medical experience to identify themselves. Chaplains were assisting the wounded. Some were holding IV bags in the air, others praying, comforting and encouraging those injured. I moved from victim to victim to offer support. Prayed with a few. Stayed with some till we could put them in a vehicle headed for a hospital. One black major was badly burned and his skin was hanging off his arm. It was a frenzy of activity.

They asked for volunteers to gather to try to go back into the building to bring out any more survivors. Time was of the essence. I stepped forward and was made leader of team 2. No one in that group was thinking of their own safety. We were now focused on getting our comrades out of there alive and to safety. With surgical masks and gloves on we quickly moved across the road and back into the building. We could see through the smoke, but the air was thick with fumes. It was hard to breathe, but we kept moving until we emerged into the courtyard and fresh air. Firefighters were trying to put out the spread-

ing fire. No one yet knew the extent of damage or fire.

The volunteers were organized into search and rescue parties. I was now made team leader of team four. Each of us shook hands and introduced ourselves by our first names. A two-star general was on my team, but rank or service status wasn't even a thought among us. We were American volunteers focused on only one thing, i.e., getting our folks out of a burning building alive. I was asked by our team to pray before we went in. No one asked what "faith" I was. It didn't seem to matter. I was a chaplain and I prayed for us all. Soon a firefighter yelled for our team to follow him into the building. Though we could see through the smoke, the fumes were so strong that after about a hundred feet in we had to withdraw back out into the courtyard to wait. We exited coughing and moved toward better air.

The longer we waited the more we realized the chances of getting anyone else out alive were diminishing. The fire was spreading. We had no news. Some began using their cell phones to let their loved ones know they were okay. An agent let me use his to call Carol [Jenkins's wife]. I let her know I was okay. She said to me, "I believed in my heart that you were okay and, if you were, you would be ministering to those hurt." My own emotions began to rise and I couldn't talk more to her. I knew from my Viet Nam and Desert Shield & Storm experiences that I needed to keep my own emotions in check and my mind focused on the mission at hand. That mission to me was twofold: one, inspire those around me to hope and, two,

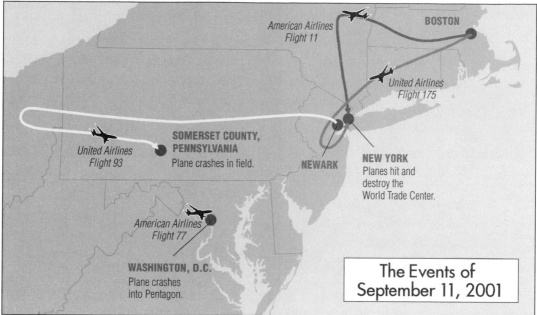

American Airlines
Flight 11

BOSTON

United Airlines
Flight 175

United Airlines
Flight 93

SOMERSET COUNTY,
PENNSYLVANIA
Plane crashes in field.

NEWARK

NEW YORK
Planes hit and
destroy the
World Trade Center.

American Airlines
Flight 77

WASHINGTON, D.C.
Plane crashes
into Pentagon.

The Events of
September 11, 2001

to do what I could to help. I dismissed the thought of what if none of us here could get out of the courtyard alive. Me saying to those around me to "stay focused on our task" helped me to stay focused as well. It was about 3 PM now, the fire was still spreading and we wcrc still waiting. Waiting was getting harder to do.

I went over to the folks responsible for setting up a temporary mortuary on the far side of the courtyard. They were anxious too. One soldier shared her concern about her son coming home and seeing that she wasn't there. I offered words of encouragement, support and prayer. They were all grateful and said so. I moved back to my group as we were now told that we were now going to have to move through the building to the blast side. Our anxiety rose.

A firefighter who knew the way led us back into the building. We could still see through smoke, but the fumes were worse. It was a very long and winding walk and I had no idea where in the Pentagon we now were, but we kept moving. At one point we had to turn around and go a different direction. Some voiced concern that we might be lost, but no one panicked. We stayed together and kept moving through the smoke. As we went by the Army Chief of Chaplains office I instinctively gave a thumbs up. I heard several behind me chokingly utter, "Hooah." I didn't look back. We kept moving. Breathing through the wet towel around my face helped a little, but when we finally emerged out the other side of the building I joined the others who were coughing out the smoke. It was awful.

Moving around to the side of the Pentagon we could now clearly see the impact area to the outside of the building. We were awestruck as we joined the thousands of other people looking on. No one could believe this was actually happening. Moving into place to wait to be called forth, folks shouted words of comfort and support to us. Bottles of water were passed our way. I saw some of my fellow chaplains and left my team for a few minutes to greet my brothers. They were as stunned as we were, but were already actively providing ministry all over the grounds. After about 30 minutes, 16 teams of 12 each volunteers moved into place to attempt to enter the building from the impact side to rescue any survivors. I was now leader of team 4. We were instructed to not lose sight of the buddy we

were paired under any circumstances. I asked a blessing upon our team. We were ready. Emotions were high. It was now about 5 PM. Just before we were going to be led in, LTG [Lieutenant General] Van Alstyne came over and asked for the volunteer leaders to huddle around him. We did.

LTG Van Alstyne thanked us for volunteering and for what each of us was willing to do, but we were not going to now be needed. He said it was much too dangerous, we didn't have the proper safety equipment and enough search and rescue workers were now on the scene. He told us that probably no one

A huge gash marks the devastation caused by an airliner that crashed into the Pentagon.

else would be thanking us, but he thanked us for what we were willing to risk for others. He told us the Old Guard [a military search and rescue unit] was arriving to assume responsibility for the operation along with the other various agencies responsible. As we dispersed he recognized me and stopped to speak to me. It was good to see him in charge.

Now the Old Guard had the mission to bring out remains. It was no longer being considered a rescue operation. No one believed anyone could still be alive in the intense heat, smoke and toxic fumes. Still some were hopeful, praying. One young soldier told me his fiancee was on the phone talking to her friend and suddenly screamed and then the phone went dead. He said he believed she saw the plane just before it hit near the window of her office. . . . He said he knew she was dead, but he wanted to join the mortuary team and go in to help retrieve her body. I asked if she was a Christian and he said that she was and so was he. We talked about the eternal hope we Christians have in Christ and the resurrection yet to come. He was comforted and so was I. . . .

I reported to the Chaplain's tent. The Military District of Washington (MDW) Command Chaplain was in charge of ministry operations on the grounds. He welcomed my help. I walked among the various types of workers—police, fire, rescue—offering words of support and encouragement. I was surprised at how many voiced their thanks and appreciation that chaplains were so visible and directly involved. As I visited the soldiers setting up mortuary affairs, I was asked to help and so agreed. A civilian there

who had been a soldier in Korea said his girlfriend had been in the area of the blast. He didn't think she was alive, but he wanted to help bring her remains out. Understandable, but I knew that was not going to be permitted. An emotional reaction could jeopardize the safety of the whole team. We stood silently together still staring in disbelief at the burning building for a long time.

Teams were now formed to go into the building to remove bodies. There were four of us chaplains. After the FBI would photograph and tag the remains inside the building and indicate location found, the Old Guard soldiers would put the remains into body bags, two chaplains (Protestant and Catholic) would pray a blessing over the remains before they were carried out of the building to a refrigeration truck waiting with a medical team and chaplain inside. A doctor would pronounce death and, after that the remains would be escorted to a controlled FBI holding area at the end of the Pentagon. Respect for the dead and chain of custody were of paramount importance. I was designated the Protestant Chaplain and Chaplain Rick Spenser designated the Catholic Chaplain who would pray over the remains inside the building. Both of us could feel the weight of the responsibility, but both of us also found relief and strength through prayer and the knowledge that what we were doing for the living and the dead was necessary and a sacred honor.

Father Spenser and I hit it off instantly. I could sense in his demeanor a quiet confidence and see in his eyes deep spiritual strength. Neither of us knew what we were

An aerial view of the Pentagon depicts the airliner's point of impact (lower left corner).

getting into, nor just how much we ourselves would need God's grace and strength in order to provide meaningful and effective ministry to those assembled around us. We walked among the soldiers listening, offering words of encouragement and hope, praying with some and silently praying for all and for each other. The fire continued to consume and nightfall was upon us when we were told there would be no entering the building tonight. After being told to report back at 0700 the next morning, Chaplain Spenser and I looked for something to eat as we headed to the MDW Chaplain operations tent.

It was now 2220 [10:20 P.M.] hours. I was exhausted and very aware of the intense pain in my left heel and in my right calf. I hadn't noticed I was limping till someone asked if I was okay. Someone else gave me a sandwich to eat and a bottle of water. I couldn't remember how many bottles of water I had already consumed, but I needed a few more. I kept my black sweater on all day because I didn't have all the stuff that goes on the military shirt. That made me sweat more, but also provided additional protection. Besides, I was in the military and was not about to appear disrespectful at a time like this.

I started walking toward my hotel (Sheraton National near the Marine Corps Barracks at Henderson Hall, about a mile), but the pain in my foot and leg wouldn't allow me to get very far. A policeman offered me a ride and I took it. Glad I did because up the hill I would have had to walk through hundreds of media folks spread across the hill. I thanked the officer and limped up the walkway. My Master Sergeant saw me and headed toward me. She hugged me and was so relieved to see me because she didn't know if I had made it out for sure. It was a touching moment, but I felt bad I had caused her so much additional worry. I told her to go ahead and drive with the Navy Chief back to South Carolina, but to be careful.

My room was as I had left it at 0700 in the morning. It had not been cleaned because the FBI locked down the top floors and put snipers on the roof. All the cleaning teams were confined to the first floor. Made sense. No one knew what was happening or what could happen next. What a day. I called the desk and they sent up some towels. I was a mess. Sunburned, dirty, exhausted and still stunned by the day's events. After a long hot shower, I listened to eleven voice messages on my room phone. I called Carol and told her I was okay, but continue to pray because we didn't know what tomorrow would bring. I couldn't talk more. It was midnight and I fell asleep.

Excerpted from "Pentagon Attack 11 September 2001," by Robert J. Jenkins, www.korea.army.mil. Copyright © 2001 by Robert J. Jenkins. Reprinted with permission.

Chapter Two

America's Response

In the first hours and days after the attacks of September 11, 2001, most Americans remained shocked. New Yorkers, in particular, were stunned by the hole the fallen towers had left in the city's skyline. One New York radio commentator said September 11 was the worst day in the city's history. Indeed, as several news reporters pointed out, it was the deadliest day on American soil since the Civil War.

Almost immediately, President George W. Bush and New York City mayor Rudy Guiliani stepped forward and provided leadership. Both men remained visible during the early days of the crisis. Bush gave several speeches following September 11 in which he reassured Americans that the full resources of the U.S. government would be used to find the people responsible

for the attacks. He also created the Office of Homeland Security, a new cabinet position whose mission is to protect the United States against future terrorist attacks. Guiliani, whose term expired December 31, 2001, often appeared at Ground Zero, the site where the World Trade Center Towers once stood. His presence there reassured and comforted many New Yorkers.

Ordinary Americans were also eager to help. The American Red Cross received so many offers of blood donations that it had to turn people away. An unprecedented outpouring of contributions flowed into numerous charities set up to help the families of victims. In the first week after the attacks, scores of charities, including the Red Cross, the September 11 Fund, and the Liberty Fund, had received pledges and donations of more than

$200 million, an amount that soared to approximately $1.5 billion by the end of the year. Whether with money, blood donations, or solid leadership, Americans and their elected officials, although shocked and saddened, responded to the September 11 attacks by being ready and willing to help wherever they could.

The President Addresses the Nation

George W. Bush, the forty-third president of the United States, was visiting a Florida elementary school when the World Trade Center and the Pentagon were attacked by terrorists. Shortly after his return to the White House, Bush spoke to the nation. Excerpted below is the speech in which he consoles Americans and reassures them that the United States will recover from the attack.

Today, our fellow citizens, our way of life, our very freedom came under attack in a series of deliberate and deadly terrorist acts. The victims were in airplanes, or in their offices; secretaries, businessmen and women, military and federal workers; moms and dads, friends and neighbors. Thousands of lives were suddenly ended by evil, despicable acts of terror.

The pictures of airplanes flying into buildings, fires burning, huge structures collapsing, have filled us with disbelief, terrible sadness, and a quiet, unyielding anger. These acts of mass murder were intended to frighten our nation into chaos and retreat. But they have failed; our country is strong.

A great people has been moved to defend a great nation. Terrorist attacks can shake the foundations of our biggest buildings, but they cannot touch the foundation of America. These acts shattered steel, but they cannot dent the steel of American resolve.

President George W. Bush arrives in Washington, D.C., before addressing the nation about the terrorist attacks on America.

America was targeted for attack because we're the brightest beacon for freedom and opportunity in the world. And no one will keep that light from shining.

Today, our nation saw evil, the very worst of human nature. And we responded with the best of America—with the daring of our rescue workers, with the caring for strangers and neighbors who came to give blood and help in any way they could.

Immediately following the first attack, I implemented our government's emergency response plans. Our military is powerful, and it's prepared. Our emergency teams are working in New York City and Washington, D.C., to help with local rescue efforts.

Our first priority is to get help to those who have been injured, and to take every precaution to protect our citizens at home and around the world from further attacks.

The functions of our government continue without interruption. Federal agencies in Washington which had to be evacuated today are reopening for essential personnel tonight, and will be open for business tomorrow. Our financial institutions remain strong, and the American economy will be open for business, as well.

The search is under way for those who are behind these evil acts. I've directed the full resources of our intelligence and law enforcement communities to find those responsible and to bring them to justice. We will make no distinction between the terrorists who committed these acts and those who harbor them.

I appreciate so very much the members of Congress who have joined me in strongly condemning these attacks. And on behalf of the American people, I thank the many world leaders who have called to offer their condolences and assistance.

America and our friends and allies join with all those who want peace and security in the world, and we stand together to win the war against terrorism. Tonight, I ask for your prayers for all those who grieve, for the children whose worlds have been shattered, for all whose sense of safety and security has been threatened. And I pray they will be comforted by a power greater than any of us, spoken through the ages in Psalm 23: "Even though I walk through the valley of the shadow of death, I fear no evil, for You are with me."

This is a day when all Americans from every walk of life unite in our resolve for justice and peace. America has stood down enemies before, and we will do so this time. None of us will ever forget this day. Yet, we go forward to defend freedom and all that is good and just in our world.

From "Statement by the President in His Address to the Nation," by George W. Bush, September 11, 2001.

 ## Our Darkest Day, Our Finest Hour

New York City was devastated by the attacks on the World Trade Center. The Twin Towers, once a seemingly invincible symbol of the city, lay in ruins, and thousands of people were dead or missing. In his weekly column, New York City mayor Rudy Guiliani discusses the tragedy.

On September 11, New York City suffered the darkest day in our long history. The destruction of the World Trade Center, and the resulting loss of thousands of lives, has broken our City's heart. But our heart still beats and our City remains strong. We will emerge from this stronger than we have ever been before.

This vicious, unprovoked attack on our City, and our Nation, demonstrates the depths of human cowardice and cruelty. Yet the reaction of New Yorkers to this tragedy has shown us the heights of human generosity and courage. Within moments after the first plane struck, ordinary men and women showed extraordinary bravery in assisting one another to safety, even at the cost of their own lives. Our Fire Fighters and Police Officers have personified courage, and though the losses to their ranks have been terrible, they have set the example for the rest of us by continuing to work with renewed vigor.

The Fire Department, in particular, has suffered greatly. More than 300 members of the Department are dead or missing as of this writing, and we have already held funerals for three of the most beloved and valued members of New York's Bravest: Chief Peter Ganci; First Deputy Commissioner William Feehan; and Father Mychal Judge. These legendary leaders and their many courageous fallen colleagues will never be forgotten.

This tragedy, along with the nearly simultaneous bombing of the Pentagon in Washington and the crash of a hijacked commercial plane near Pittsburgh, has touched

New York City mayor Rudy Guiliani consoled New Yorkers and urged them to remain strong.

the lives of millions of people throughout our City, across the Nation, and around the world. Family members, friends, and co-workers have been suddenly taken from us. This enormous loss provokes our sadness, and it also stirs a sense of outrage and anger. President Bush is right to call this an act of war. He is also right to declare that the terrorist enemies of the United States will face retaliation. Basic justice—and the national interest—demand no less.

Yet even as we mourn our dead and prepare for what could be a long and bitter war against an elusive enemy, let us always remember that our greatest national strengths are our openness, our diversity, our inclusiveness, and our freedom. These are the assets that our terrorist foes seek to destroy, but these are also the values that will guarantee our eventual and total victory. The people of the City of New York will demonstrate that we are stronger than these barbarians. We are not going to participate in group blame or group hatred, because those are the sicknesses that caused this tragedy. Our City is going to continue to honor its immigrant heritage. Through the strength of our example, we are going to send the message that life in our City goes on, undeterred. We will continue to embody the highest ideals of America.

I have always had full confidence in the people of this City, and that confidence has risen even higher as I have watched the behavior of New Yorkers in the wake of this tragedy. They evacuated the scene of destruction in good order; they almost immediately formed long lines to donate blood; they have made generous corporate and individual donations of money and supplies; they have offered welcome encouragement and solace to the relatives of the missing and to our exhausted rescue workers. We are a united City, and I have never been so proud to be a New Yorker.

From "Our Darkest Day; Our Finest Hour," by Rudy Guiliani, Mayor's Weekly Column, September 24, 2001.

 ## America Has Withstood This Attack

The terrorist attacks on the World Trade Center, the Pentagon, and Flight 93 were unprecedented in American history. Even so, say the editors of the Los Angeles Times *in the following excerpt, America and democracy continue to stand strong.*

On Tuesday [September 11, 2001], civilization's modern nightmare materialized as terrorists attacked American cities, destroying national landmarks and exacting a terrible human toll. But even as smoke billowed across Manhattan and dust settled over Washington, this mighty nation was shaking off the massive blow.

Buildings collapsed. Democracy stands.

The tragedy unfolded on live television, offering the world a lesson in courage and resolve. As terror and chaos advanced, determined forces stepped forward to restore calm.

The treacherous acts of demented minds led to families shattered, dreams crushed, loves lost—the unwritten futures canceled by cruelty. Immediately, though, came America's reaction. Rescuers charged into doomed buildings. Police braved falling debris to aid the wounded. Reporters sought to sort rumor from fact. Pilots diverted planes and landed safely.

Evil attacked. The people withstood the assault.

Those shocking images of smoke and dust come down to this: A father, gone. A wife. A brother. Gone as utterly as the famous towers in which they worked. Gone, too, the passengers and airline crews en route to California and elsewhere.

Nationwide, people swarm blood banks, eager to have their own blood flow into the veins of those wounded by an unknown enemy. Let that enemy note that this nation of many peoples is often at odds within itself but under pressure is united; a blow against one is a blow against all.

A Watershed in the Lives of America's Children

For many parents, the most indelible image will not be of a plane smashing into a building but of children's faces as they grapple with that image, one that shattered the world they thought they knew. For a generation of young

A child waves an American flag above a crowd of mourners who gathered to honor victims of the September 11 attacks.

people, this is their Pearl Harbor; their Kennedy assassination. Adults surely felt that old fear rising. But across the country they slung arms around children and shared with them a wisdom taught by past tragedies. "Yes, you just witnessed evil," they told the innocents. "But take heart, our world will survive."

Tuesday's attack struck at the heart of America's original melting pot, the city where for more than a hundred years people from every culture and every corner of the world have come seeking refuge, freedom and a better life. For millions, the first glimpse they got of this nation as they entered New York Harbor was the Statue of Liberty holding aloft her torch as a beacon of tolerance and freedom. These immigrants and their descendants—of every religion, race and ethnicity—have made the United States the world's most powerful nation and simultaneously its most tolerant.

Here in Los Angeles, too, our neighbors are from every corner of this troubled planet. As we garner strength by joining together in rage and sorrow, the world will see that the great experiment—*e pluribus unum* [out of many, one]—continues. One way it will continue will be for Americans to refrain from blaming groups for the evil acts of individuals. There must be no finger-pointing based on ethnicity or religion. If Americans turn on each other, those behind the heinous acts will be the winners.

America has been fortunate. Foreign enemies have, until now, caused little loss of life on our mainland. The bloodshed of the War for Independence paved the way for the establishment of a new nation. The traumatic mayhem of the Civil War was self-inflicted.

One of the hallmarks of World War II was that, with the exception of the Pearl Harbor attack, the United States didn't live through the bitter experience of the warring European nations. For the United States, battles happened somewhere else.

Never again can this nation be quite so secure. Tuesday was a day that changed America. Just as national reorientations were required after the sinking in 1915 of the ocean liner Lusitania and after Pearl Harbor, Tuesday's attack will also change this nation.

The United States' resilience stems in part from the nation's ability to adapt. We will question what more could have been done to protect our people. We will hold accountable any who fell short in their duties. Yes, we wonder how airport safety shields could be so porous, how we could have had so little inkling of what was to come.

Terrorism has been a domestic threat for years, and yet the last FBI director identified it when he left his post as a critical concern that is still unsatisfactorily addressed.

For the moment, however, Americans are unified, looking forward. The nation could be confident that it would rebuild even as the first terrorist fires raged.

Already leaders promise that government agencies, which had to be evacuated, will reopen for essential business and that financial markets will resume doing business calmly. This is a tall order, but one that must be fulfilled.

The President Must Rise to His Greatest Challenge

When we inaugurate presidents, we ask them to support and defend the Constitution against all enemies foreign and domestic. President Bush is undergoing his toughest test and must rise to it. He made a good first step Tuesday evening when, back in Washington, he addressed the nation. He said: "These acts of mass murder were intended to frighten our nation into chaos and retreat. But they have failed. Our country is strong. A great people has been moved to defend a great nation. Terrorist attacks can shake the foundations of our biggest buildings, but they cannot touch the foundation of America. These acts shatter steel, but they cannot dent the steel of American resolve."

Bush also identified the day's clearest heroes. "Today, our nation saw evil, the very worst of human nature, and we responded with the best of America, with the daring of our rescue workers, with the caring for strangers and neighbors who came to give blood and help in any way they could." That includes the many firefighters in New York who perished in brave attempts to save lives.

America will react, but it must do so with certainty, not guesswork, and the resolve that goes with confidence. The nation's leaders will determine who is responsible and do whatever is necessary to make sure the threat is removed. Bush importantly vowed to find and punish not just the terrorists but their backers. The decision he and Congress have to face is whether the U.S. reaction will, as in previous terrorist attacks, concentrate on legal remedies or on military retaliation or some combination. . . .

There will be speculations and cynicism, denunciations and denials, revelations and ruminations, accusations and anger all over this land in coming days. But out of this nationwide emotional incoherence must come—will come—that democratic resolve so familiar to Americans and their friends—and so ominous to this nation's enemies.

Los Angeles Times, "U.S. Resolve: Unshattered," September 12, 2001, p. B-8.

 ## They Were Heroes Every Day

A month after the September 11 terrorist attacks, Secretary of Defense Donald H. Rumsfeld, spoke at a memorial service at the Pentagon honoring the military and civilian workers and the airline passengers and crew who were killed at the site. In his speech, Rumsfeld asserts that the victims were heroes to their families and friends long before they gave their lives on September 11, 2001.

We are gathered here because of what happened here on September 11th. Events that bring to mind tragedy—but also our gratitude to those who came to assist that day and afterwards, those we saw at the Pentagon site every day—the guards, police, fire and rescue workers, the Defense Protective service, hospitals, Red Cross, family center professionals and volunteers and many others.

And yet our reason for being here today is something else.

We are gathered here to remember, to console and to pray.

To remember comrades and colleagues, friends and family members—those lost to us on Sept. 11th.

A somber American president attends a memorial service for those who died at the Pentagon on September 11.

We remember them as heroes. And we are right to do so. They died because—in words of justification offered by their attackers—they were Americans. They died, then, because of how they lived—as free men and women, proud of their freedom, proud of their country and proud of their country's cause—the cause of human freedom.

And they died for another reason—the simple fact they worked here in this building—the Pentagon.

It is seen as a place of power, the locus of command for what has been called the greatest accumulation of military might in history. And yet a might used far differently than the long course of history has usually known.

In the last century, this building existed to oppose two totalitarian regimes that sought to oppress and to rule other nations. And it is no exaggeration of historical judgment to say that without this building, and those who worked here, those two regimes would not have been stopped or thwarted in their oppression of countless millions.

But just as those regimes sought to rule and oppress, others in this century seek to do the same by corrupting a noble religion. Our President has been right to see the similarity—and to say that the fault, the evil is the same. It is the will to power, the urge to dominion over others, to the point of oppressing them, even to taking thousands of innocent lives—or more. And that this oppression makes the terrorist a believer—not in the theology of God, but the theology of self—and in the whispered words of temptation: "Ye shall be as Gods."

In targeting this place, then, and those who worked here, the attackers, the evildoers correctly sensed that the opposite of all they were, and stood for, resided here.

Those who worked here—those who on Sept. 11 died here—whether civilians or in uniform,—side by side they sought not to rule, but to serve. They sought not to oppress, but to liberate. They worked not to take lives, but to protect them. And they tried not to preempt God, but see to it His creatures lived as He intended—in the light and dignity of human freedom.

Our first task then is to remember the fallen as they were—as they would have wanted to be remembered—living in freedom, blessed by it, proud of it and willing—like so many others before them, and like so many today, to die for it.

And to remember them as believers in the heroic ideal for which this nation stands and for which this building exists—the ideal of service to country and to others.

Beyond all this, their deaths remind us of a new kind of evil, the evil of a threat and menace to which this nation and the world has now fully awakened, because of them.

In causing this awakening, then, the terrorists have assured their own destruction. And those we mourn today, have, in the moment of their death, assured their own triumph over hate and fear. For out of this act of terror—and the awakening it brings—here and across the globe—will surely come a victory over terrorism. A victory that one day may save millions from the harm of weapons of mass destruction. And this victory—their victory—we pledge today.

But if we gather here to remember them—we are also here to console those who shared their lives, those who loved them. And yet, the irony is that those whom we have come to console have given us the best of all consolations, by reminding us not only of the meaning of the deaths, but of the lives of their loved ones.

"He was a hero long before the eleventh of September," said a friend of one of those we have lost—"a hero every single day, a hero to his family, to his friends and to his professional peers."

A veteran of the Gulf War—hardworking, who showed up at the Pentagon at 3:30 in the morning, and then headed home in the afternoon to be with his children.

About him and those who served with him, his wife said: "It's not just when a plane hits their building. They are heroes every day."

"Heroes every day." We are here to affirm that. And to do this on behalf of America.

And also to say to those who mourn, who have lost loved ones: Know that the heart of America is here today, and that it speaks to each one of you words of sympathy, consolation, compassion and love. All the love that the heart of America—and a great heart it is—can muster.

Watching and listening today, Americans everywhere are saying: I wish I could be there to tell them how sorry we are, how much we grieve for them. And to tell them too, how thankful we are for those they loved, and that we will remember them, and recall always the meaning of their deaths and their lives.

A Marine chaplain, in trying to explain why there could be no human explanation for a tragedy such as this, said once: "You would think it would break the heart of God."

We stand today in the midst of tragedy—the mystery of tragedy. Yet a mystery that is part of that larger awe and wonder that causes us to bow our heads in faith and say of those we mourn, those we have lost, the words of scripture: "Lord now let Thy servants go in peace, Thy word has been fulfilled."

To the families and friends of our fallen colleagues and comrades we extend today our deepest sympathy and condolences—and those of the American people.

We pray that God will give some share of the peace that now belongs to those we lost, to those who knew and loved them in this life.

But as we grieve together we are also thankful—thankful for their lives, thankful for the time we had with them. And proud too—as proud as they were—that they lived their lives as Americans.

We are mindful too—and resolute that their deaths, like their lives, shall have meaning. And that the birthright of human freedom—a birthright that was theirs as Americans and for which they died—will always be ours and our children's. And through our efforts and example, one day, the birthright of every man, woman, and child on earth.

Excerpted from remarks prepared for delivery by Secretary of Defense Donald H. Rumsfeld at the Pentagon, Arlington VA, October 11, 2001.

The Faces of the Missing

Thousands of people were killed when the World Trade Center towers collapsed, buried under tons of rubble and debris. Yet many of the victims' families and friends clung to the belief that their loved ones had managed to escape the towers and were still alive. Near the towers was a site where posters and signs—featuring photos of the missing—were displayed, in the hopes that they might be recognized and found. Below, the editors of the monthly magazine Mortgage Wire *urge New York City officials to allow the posters to remain.*

It's hard to read the names, which firm in the World Trade Center they worked for, which floor they were on. But we hope the city fathers let the flyers stay up awhile, even though the chance of finding the people in them safe is slight.

That's because these postings are a way of making the vanished reappear, of finding the missing, in a sense, by identifying them through a few essentials: what their names were, where they worked and who they worked for, who they loved.

The pictures on the flyers are invariably beautiful, and they display the enduring innocence and the moral integrity of people going about the . . . business of their lives. The loved ones are showcased in all their vitality and presence. They are not missing in these photos.

These remarkable flyers are not just requests for help. They are also requests to remember, and to appreciate. The photos in them are eloquent statements of pride in the person who is gone. They are reassuring statements of normalcy from a different world than this disorienting new one. They are heartwrenching statements that rise to a simple question: How could this awful thing happen, and why to them?

We who pass by recognize the faces of the missing. They are people we have seen on the street, in the office, on the train going home, and in the parks and on the lawns of summer.

There is a lot of ourselves in these pictures, and their mirror-like qualities can be disturbing. The people in them are our age, and their kids look like ours, and they worked in the field we cover. Inevitably they are marked "Missing," and that's about us as well as them. We are missing them and an essential piece of our lives that's been suddenly and violently wrenched away.

These unbearably poignant snapshots are a way of making the dimensions of the

Pictures and descriptions of the World Trade Center's missing and dead cover a bus shelter in New York City.

disaster real, of fixing it in our memory. And memory is one way of finding and keeping the missing. At the recent telethon fundraiser for the victims of the attack, for instance, the rock musician Sting spoke so warmly of his friend Herman Sandler, the co-founder of Sandler O'Neill Mortgage Finance, that we thought we knew Mr. Sandler, and wished we had.

By keeping these remarkable pictures in mind, a new picture of the tragedy comes to mind. It's clear the only thing that collapsed on Sept. 11 was metal and concrete, not the people within. Given the strong foundations of the missing peoples' lives we've been privileged to get a glimpse of, they did not fall when the floors gave way. We think they rose instead, with the smoke that rose on that sunny day, and from those high towers they must have had a considerable head start towards the heavens.

From "The Faces of the Missing," *Mortgage Wire*, October 10, 2001. Copyright © 2001 by *Mortgage Wire*. Reprinted with permission.

Chapter Three

Response from Abroad

The grief and outrage Americans expressed after the September 11, 2001, attacks was to be expected. For many, similar international responses, however, were a surprise. With only a few exceptions, political leaders and ordinary people around the world reacted to the terrorist attacks with anger, sadness, and resolve. Russian President Vladimir Putin, for example, denounced the attacks and urged the world community to unite and fight terrorism together. Likewise, Italy's minister of foreign affairs, Renato Ruggiero, argued that the attacks against the United States had attacked the values held by most countries around the world. By far, though, the strongest show of support came from Great Britain's prime minister Tony Blair, who called terrorism a world evil and vowed to assist the United States in its military response. Further, only a

week after the attacks, Blair and his wife flew to New York City to attend a memorial service for the thousands killed.

Ordinary citizens of countries like Russia, Italy, and Great Britain echoed their leaders' response. At the American embassy in Moscow, mourners left bouquets of flowers. Across Europe, residents expressed condolences to Americans they met on the street. And in London, hundreds participated in an official day of mourning.

America found allies in unlikely places as well. Leaders in countries like Pakistan and Egypt, places whose political views and way of life differ greatly from that of the United States, expressed grief and solidarity as well. Egyptian president Hosni Mubarak called the attack "a wake-up call for all of humanity." And Pakistani president General Pervez Musharraf agreed to help the

U.S. government search out the terrorists responsible.

There were critics, of course; Iraq's Saddam Hussein, in particular, often gave speeches that sounded unsympathetic to the victims. However, most people around the world reacted to the September 11 attacks in much the same way: with sorrow, anger, and a determination to catch and punish the people responsible.

We Must Act to Protect the Living

Tony Blair, Great Britain's prime minister, spoke to the House of Commons, a division of the country's legislature, on September 14, 2001, three days after the terrorist attacks against America. In his speech, excerpted below, Blair emphasizes that the September 11 attacks were not just against the United States, but against the entire free world.

These attacks were not just attacks upon people and buildings; nor even merely upon the USA; these were attacks on the basic democratic values in which we all believe so passionately and on the civilised world. . . .

What happened in the United States on Tuesday was an act of wickedness for which there can never be justification. Whatever the cause, whatever the perversion of religious feeling, whatever the political belief, to inflict such terror on the world; to take the lives of so many innocent and defenceless men, women, and children, can never ever be justified.

Let us unite too, with the vast majority of decent people throughout the world, in sending our condolences to the government and the people of America. They are our friends and allies. We the British are a people that stand by our friends in time of need, trial and tragedy, and we do so without hesitation now. . . .

There are three things we must now take forward urgently.

First, we must bring to justice those responsible. Rightly, President Bush and the US Government have proceeded with care. They did not lash out. They did not strike first and think afterwards. Their very deliberation is a measure of the seriousness of their intent.

They, together with allies, will want to identify, with care, those responsible. This is a judgement that must and will be based on hard evidence.

Once that judgement is made, the appropriate action can be taken. It will be determined, it will take time, it will continue over time until this menace is properly dealt with and its machinery of terror destroyed.

But one thing should be very clear. By their acts, these terrorists and those behind them have made themselves the enemies of the civilised world.

The objective will be to bring to account those who have organised, aided, abetted and incited this act of infamy [evil, criminal]; and those that harbour or help them have a choice: either to cease their protection of our enemies; or be treated as an enemy themselves.

Secondly, this is a moment when every difference between nations, every divergence of interest, every irritant in our relations, are put to one side in one common endeavour. The world should stand together against this outrage.

NATO has already, for the first time since it was founded in 1949, invoked Article 5 and determined that this attack in America will be considered as an attack against the Alliance as a whole.

The UN Security Council on Wednesday passed a resolution which set out its readiness to take all necessary steps to combat terrorism.

From Russia, China, the EU, from Arab states, from Asia and the Americas, from every continent of the world has come united condemnation. This solidarity should be maintained and translated into support for action.

We do not yet know the exact origin of this evil. But, if, as appears likely, it is so-called Islamic fundamentalists, we know they do not speak or act for the vast majority of decent law-abiding Muslims throughout the world. I say to our Arab and Muslim friends: neither you nor Islam is responsible for this; on the contrary, we know you share our shock at this terrorism; and we ask you as friends to make common cause with us in defeating this barbarism that is totally foreign to the true spirit and teachings of Islam.

And I would add that, now more than ever, we have reason not to let the Middle East Peace Process slip still further but if at all possible to reinvigorate it and move it forward.

Thirdly, whatever the nature of the immediate response to these terrible events in America, we need to re-think dramatical-ly the scale and nature of the action the world takes to combat terrorism.

We know a good deal about many of these terror groups. But as a world we have not been effective at dealing with them.

And of course it is difficult. We are democratic. They are not. We have respect for human life. They do not. We hold essentially

British prime minister, Tony Blair, urges the nations of the world to fight terrorism.

liberal values. They do not. As we look into these issues it is important that we never lose sight of our basic values. But we have to understand the nature of the enemy and act accordingly.

Civil liberties are a vital part of our country, and of our world. But the most basic liberty of all is the right of the ordinary citizen to go about their business free from fear or terror. That liberty has been denied, in the cruellest way imaginable, to the passengers aboard the hijacked planes, to those who perished in the trade towers and the Pentagon, to the hundreds of rescue workers killed as they tried to help.

So we need to look once more: nationally and internationally at extradition laws, and the mechanisms for international justice; at how these terrorist groups are financed and their money laundered: and the links between terror and crime and we need to frame a response that will work, and hold internationally.

For this form of terror knows no mercy; no pity, and it knows no boundaries.

And let us make this reflection. A week ago, anyone suggesting terrorists would kill thousands of innocent people in downtown New York would have been dismissed as alarmist. It happened. We know that these groups are fanatics, capable of killing without discrimination. The limits on the numbers they kill and their methods of killing are not governed by morality. The limits are only practical or technical. We know, that they would, if they could, go further and use chemical or biological or even nuclear weapons of mass destruction. We know, also,

that there are groups or people, occasionally states, who trade the technology and capability for such weapons.

It is time this trade was exposed, disrupted, and stamped out. We have been warned by the events of 11 September. We should act on the warning.

So there is a great deal to do and many details to be filled in, much careful work to be undertaken over the coming days, weeks and months.

We need to mourn the dead; and then act to protect the living.

Terrorism has taken on a new and frightening aspect.

The people perpetrating it wear the ultimate badge of the fanatic: they are prepared to commit suicide in pursuit of their beliefs.

Our beliefs are the very opposite of the fanatics. We believe in reason, democracy and tolerance.

These beliefs are the foundation of our civilised world. They are enduring, they have served us well and as history has shown we have been prepared to fight, when necessary to defend them. But the fanatics should know: we hold these beliefs every bit as strongly as they hold theirs.

Now is the time to show it.

Excerpted from "We Need to Mourn the Dead; and Then Act to Protect the Living," by Tony Blair, Statement by the Prime Minister, September 14, 2001. www.pm.gov.uk.

 ## The World Has Been Attacked

Jean Chrétien is the prime minister of Canada, another close friend and ally of the United States. In this excerpt of Chrétien's

speech to the Canadian legislature, the prime minister argues that the terrorist attacks against the United States also threaten Canada and the rest of the world.

There are those rare occasions when time seems to stand still. When a singular event transfixes the world. There are also those terrible occasions when the dark side of human nature escapes civilized restraint and shows its ugly face to a stunned world.

Tuesday, September 11, 2001, will forever be etched in memory as a day when time stood still.

Mr. Speaker, when I saw the scenes of devastation my first thoughts and words were for all the victims and the American people. But there are no words, in any language, whose force or eloquence could equal the quiet testimony last Friday of 100,000 Canadians gathered just a few yards from here for our National Day of Mourning.

I was proud to be one of them. And I was equally proud of the Canadians who gathered in ceremonies right across the country.

It was a sea of sorrow and sympathy for those who have lost friends and loved ones— Americans, Canadians, citizens of many countries. Above all, it was a sea of solidarity [unity] with our closest friend and partner in the world: the United States of America.

Mr. Speaker, as always, this time of crisis brought out the very best in our people. From prayer meetings and vigils. To the countless numbers who lined up to give blood. From a flood of donations by individuals and businesses. To patience in the face of delays and

inconvenience. And we were all moved by the sight of Canadians opening up their hearts and their homes to thousands of confused and anxious air travellers who had no place to go. . . .

The House must also address the threat that terrorism poses to all civilized peoples and the role that Canada must play in defeating it.

To understand what is at stake, we need only reflect on the symbolic meaning of the World Trade Center Towers. In the words of their architect, the Towers were *"a representation of our [America's] belief in humanity, our need for individual dignity, our belief in cooperation and, through cooperation, our ability to find greatness."*

So let us be clear: this was not just an attack on the United States. These cold-blooded killers struck a blow at the values and beliefs of free and civilized people everywhere.

The world has been attacked. The world must respond. Because we are at war against terrorism and Canada—a nation founded on a belief in freedom, justice and tolerance—will be part of that response.

Terrorists are not attached to any one country. Terrorism is a global threat. The perpetrators have demonstrated their ability to move with ease from country to country. From place to place. To make use of the freedom and openness of the victims on whom they prey. The very freedom and openness that we cherish and will protect.

They are willing, indeed anxious, to die in the commission of their crimes and to use innocent civilians as shields and as tools.

Canadians gather to show support for their American neighbors and to honor those who died during the September 11 attacks.

We must prepare ourselves, and Canadians, for the fact that this will be a long struggle with no easy solutions. One in which patience and wisdom are essential.

But, Mr. Speaker, let us not deceive ourselves as to the nature of the threat that faces us; that it can be defeated easily or simply with one swift strike. We must be guided by a commitment to do what works in the long run not by what makes us feel better in the short run.

Mr. Speaker, our actions will be ruled by resolve. But not fear.

If laws need to be changed they will be. If security has to be increased to protect Canadians it will be. We will remain vigilant.

But we will not give into the temptation, in a rush to increase security, to undermine the values that we cherish and which have made Canada a beacon of hope, freedom and tolerance to the world. We will not be stampeded in the hope—vain and ultimately self-defeating—that we can make Canada a fortress against the world.

Finally, Mr. Speaker, I want to make another very, very important point.

Immigration is central to the Canadian experience and identity. We have welcomed people from all corners of the globe: all nationalities, colours and religions. This is who we are. And let there be no doubt: we will allow no one to force us to sacrifice our values or traditions under the pressure of urgent circumstances. We will continue to welcome people from the whole world. We will continue to offer refuge to the persecuted.

I say again: No one will stop this!

I have been saddened by the fact that the terror of last Tuesday has provoked demonstrations against Muslim Canadians and other minority groups in Canada. This is completely unacceptable. The terrorists win when they export their hatred. The evil perpetrators of this horror represent no community or religion. They stand for evil. Nothing else!

As I have said, this is a struggle against terrorism. Not against any one community or faith. Today, more than ever, we must reaffirm the fundamental values of our Charter of Rights and Freedoms: the equality of every race, every colour, every religion, and every ethnic origin.

Mr. Speaker, we are all Canadians!

We are a compassionate and righteous people. When we see the searing images of mothers and fathers. Sisters and brothers—many of them Canadian—wandering the streets of New York looking for their missing loved ones, we know where our duty lies.

We have never been a bystander in the struggle for justice in the world. We will stand with Americans. As neighbours. As

friends. As family. We will stand with our allies. We will do what we must to defeat terrorism.

But let our actions be guided by a spirit of wisdom and perseverance. By our values and our way of life.

And, as we go on with the struggle, let us never, ever, forget who we are. And what we stand for!

Excerpted from Prime Minister Jean Chrétien's "Address on the Occasion of a Special House of Commons Debate in Response to the Terrorist Attacks in the United States on September 11, 2001," September 17, 2001.

The United Nations Condemns the Terrorist Attacks

For more than fifty years, the United Nations, based in New York City, has tried to promote international peace, respect for human rights, and cooperation in solving international problems. In the following excerpt, Kofi Annan, the secretary-general of the United Nations, condemns the September 11 attacks in a speech to the General Assembly.

Our host country, and this wonderful host city that has been so good to us over five decades, have just been subjected to a terrorist attack such as we had hardly dared to imagine, even in our worst nightmares.

We are all struggling to find words to express our sense of grief and outrage, our profound sympathy for the untold numbers of injured and bereaved, and our solidarity with the people and Government of the United States in this hour of trial.

We are struggling, too, to voice our intense admiration and respect for the valiant police officers, fire fighters, and workers of all kinds who are engaged in the rescue and recovery effort—and especially for those, far too numerous, whose determination to help their fellow men and women has cost them their own lives.

We are struggling, above all, to find adequate words of condemnation for those who planned and carried out these abominable attacks.

In truth, no such words can be found. And words, in any case, are not enough.

This Assembly, Mr. President [President of the UN General Assembly], has condemned terrorism on numerous occasions. It has said repeatedly that terrorist acts are never justified, no matter what considerations may be invoked.

And it has called on all States [countries] to adopt measures, in accordance with the Charter and other relevant provisions of international law, to prevent terrorism and strengthen international cooperation against it. . . .

Earlier today, as you know, the Security Council expressed its readiness to take all necessary steps to respond to yesterday's attacks, and to combat all forms of terrorism, in accordance with its responsibilities under the Charter.

I trust that it will indeed take such steps, and that this Assembly—and all its Members—

A U.N. Security Council meeting in New York City where members condemned the September 11 attacks.

will follow suit. All nations of the world must be united in their solidarity with the victims of terrorism, and in their determination to take action—both against the terrorists themselves and against all those who give them any kind of shelter, assistance or encouragement.

I trust, Mr. President, that that message will go out loud and clear to the whole world from every Member of this Assembly, which represents the whole world.

Excerpted from "Words Alone Inadequate as Response to Terrorist Attacks, Secretary-General Tells Opening of Fifty-Sixth General Assembly," by Kofi Annan, Press Release, September 12, 2001.

 ## Pakistan Is Facing a Very Difficult Situation

When the Taliban—a group of Islamic fundamentalists—took power in Afghanistan in the mid–1990s, the government of Pakistan, an Islamic country that borders Afghanistan on the east, provided financial and military aid to the new leaders. In 2001, when the United States decided to rid Afghanistan of the Taliban and terrorists trained by Osama bin Laden, Pakistani officials were forced to decide whether or not they would continue to support the Taliban. Shortly after the attacks of September 11, 2001, Pakistan's president and military leader, Pervez Musharraf, addressed that issue in a speech to his countrymen. The United States asked for Pakistan's help in its war against bin Laden and terrorism, he says in the excerpt below, and Musharraf agreed. He asks his country's citizens to trust his decision and understand that he would never compromise Pakistan's honor and integrity.

The situation confronting the nation today and the international crisis have impelled me to take the nation into confidence.

First of all, I would like to express heartfelt sympathies to the United States for the thousands of valuable lives lost in the United States due to horrendous acts of terrorism.

We are all the more grieved because in this incident people from about 45 countries from all over the world lost their lives. People of all ages old, children, women and people from all and every religion lost their lives. Many Pakistanis also lost their lives.

These people were capable Pakistanis who had gone to improve their lives. On this loss of lives I express my sympathies with those families. I pray to Allah to rest their souls in peace.

This act of terrorism has raised a wave of deep grief, anger and retaliation in the United States. Their first target from day one is Osama bin Laden's movement Al-Qaida.

The second target are Taliban and that is because Taliban have given refuge to Osama and his network. . . . They [the United States] have been demanding their [bin Laden and al-Qaida] extradition and presentation before the international court of justice. Taliban have been rejecting this.

The third target is a long war against terrorism at the international level. The thing to ponder is that in these three targets nobody is talking about war against Islam or the people of Afghanistan.

Pakistan is being asked to support this campaign. What is this support? Generally speaking, these are three important things in which America is asking for our help.

First is intelligence and information exchange, second support is the use of our airspace and the third is that they are asking for logistic support from us.

I would like to tell you now that they do not have any operational plan right now. Therefore we do not have any details on this count but we know that whatever are the United States' intentions they have the support of the UN Security Council and the General Assembly in the form of a resolution.

This is a resolution for war against terrorism and this is a resolution for punishing those people who support terrorism. Islamic countries have supported this resolution. This is the situation as it prevailed in the outside world.

Now I would like to inform you about the internal situation. Pakistan is facing a very critical situation.... The decision we take today can have far-reaching and wide-ranging consequences.

The crisis is formidable and unprecedented. If we take wrong decisions in this crisis, it can lead to worst consequences. On the other hand, if we take right decisions, its results will be good.

The negative consequences can endanger Pakistan's integrity and solidarity. Our critical concerns, our important concerns can come under threat....

The decision should reflect supremacy of righteousness and it should be in conformity with Islam. Whatever we are doing, it is according to Islam and it upholds the principle of righteousness. I would like to say that decisions about the national interests should

be made with wisdom and rational judgement.

At this moment, it is not the question of bravery or cowardice. We are all very brave. My own response in such situations is usually of daring. But bravery without rational judgement tantamounts [is equal] to stupidity. There is no clash between bravery and sound judgement.

Allah Almighty says in the holy Quran, "The one bestowed with sagacity [insight] is the one who get a big favour from Allah." We have to take recourse to sanity. We have to save our nation from damage. We have to build up our national respect. "Pakistan comes first, everything else comes later." ...

What is the lesson for us in this? The lesson is that when there is a crisis situation, the path of wisdom is better than the path of emotions. Therefore, we have to take a strategic decision.

There is no question of weakness of faith or cowardice. For Pakistan, life can be sacrificed and I am sure every Pakistani will give his life for Pakistan. I have fought two wars. I have seen dangers. I faced them and by the grace of Allah never committed a cowardly act.

But at this time one should not bring harm to the country. We cannot make the future of a hundred and forty million people bleak. Even otherwise it is said in Shariah [Islamic law] that if there are two difficulties at a time and a selection has to be made it is better to opt for the lesser one. Some of our friends seem to be much worried about Afghanistan.

I must tell them that I and my government are much more worried about Afghanistan and Taliban. I have done everything for

Afghanistan and Taliban when the entire world is against them. I have met about twenty to twenty five world leaders and talked to each of them in favour of the Taliban. I have told them that sanctions should not be imposed on Afghanistan. . . .

I have been repeating this stance before all leaders but I am sorry to say that none of our friends accepted this.

Even in this situation, we are trying our best to cooperate with them. I sent Director General ISI with my personal letter to Mullah Umar [the Taliban leader]. He returned after spending two days there. I have informed Mullah Umar about the gravity of the situation. We are trying our best to come out of

this critical situation without any damage to Afghanistan and Taliban.

This is my earnest endeavour and with the blessings of Allah I will continue to seek such a way out. We are telling the Americans too that they should be patient. Whatever their plans, they should be cautious and balanced: We are asking them to come up with whatever evidence they have against Osama bin Laden; What I would like to know is how do we save Afghanistan and Taliban. And how do we ensure that they suffer minimum losses: I am sure that you will favour that we do so and bring some improvement by working with the nations of the world. At this juncture, I am worried about Pakistan only.

Activists from the All India Anti-Terrorist Front (AIATF) show their support for America and the fight against terrorism.

I am the Supreme Commander of Pakistan and I give top priority to the defence of Pakistan, Defence of any other country comes later. We want to take decisions in the interest of Pakistan. I know that the majority of the people favour our decisions. I also know that some elements are trying to take unfair advantage of the situation and promote their personal agenda and advance the interests of their parties. They are poised to create dissentions and damage the country.

There is no reason why this minority should be allowed to hold the sane majority as a hostage. I appeal to all Pakistanis to display unity and solidarity and foil the nefarious [evil] designs of such elements who intend to harm the interests of the country.

At this critical juncture, we have to frustrate the evil designs of our enemies and safeguard national interests. Pakistan is considered a fortress of Islam. God forbid, if this fortress is harmed in any way it would cause damage to the cause of Islam. My dear countrymen, Have trust in me. . . .

We have not compromised on national honour and integrity and I shall not disappoint you on this occasion either. This is firm pledge to you.

Excerpted from Pervez Musharraf's "Speech of President General Pervez Musharraf Broadcast on Radio and Television," September 19, 2001.

 ## What the World Must Do

On September 18, 2001, Hosni Mubarak, the president of Egypt, was interviewed by Arnaud de Borchgrave, editor at large of United Press International, about the ter-rorist attacks against the United States. In the interview excerpted below, Mubarak discusses his ideas of how to free the world of terrorism.

Q.: How do you view the enormity of the tragedy that has befallen the US, or indeed the world?

A.: It's so huge. It defies imagination. But the whole world is now involved. The casualties are from many nations. It's a wake-up call for all of humanity. We've all read intelligence reports about terrorist groups and their plans to do this and that, but absolutely nothing prepared US for hijacked civilian airliners plowing into the twin towers of the world trade centre and the pentagon, the very nerve centers of America's financial and military might. The White House itself narrowly escaped total destruction. It's a science-fiction nightmare come true.

Q.: How is this going to affect the world?

A.: Finally we're going to get really serious about transnational terrorism by decisive action rather than lip service. But we must be careful not to embark on the wrong course of action. The Bush administration's plans for a coalition of nations would simply divide the world between those who are part of the coalition and those who are not— and thus fail to reach the objective.

Q.: So what do you think is the right course?

A.: An international conference at the highest level, held at the UN to sign a solemn treaty on counter-terrorism, a document that must be well-prepared beforehand, leading to a strong binding resolution, with no wiggle room, to be implemented by all the countries in the world. This is a prerequisite if we want to live safely on this planet. . . .

Q.: And now what practical measures do you see emerging at the global counter-terrorist summit you are recommending?

A.: Those nations who ignore resolutions agreed to at such a summit, big or small, should be isolated, ostracized, boycotted.

Q.: What kind of resolutions with what practical effect?

A.: How to deal with transnational terror.

Q.: But how would you deal with it?

A.: Starting at the technical level and moving on to foreign ministers, (the counter-terrorism agreement) should be meticulously prepared for a UN Summit of Heads of State and Government.

Q.: That's still rather vague. What does your imagination tell you as to what practical steps could be taken?

A.: Not a single country would be allowed to hide terrorists who committed acts of terrorism in other countries. These terrorists now move freely from country to country with impunity [freely], making contacts, picking up money, coordinating through encrypted e-mail messages. Even your director of the National Security Agency (Gen. Mike Hayden) said (last February on CBS-TV's "60 Minutes II" program) that Osama Bin Laden's organization had managed to outplay your vast, global electronic resources.

Q.: But how does one remove Osama Bin Laden from Afghanistan?

A.: When all the nations of the world agree that no safe haven for terrorists will be tolerated, Afghanistan will have to extradite him or face a total cutoff from the assistance it is now getting from Pakistan. The three nations that now recognize the Taliban government would have to sever all ties.

Q.: A summit resolution is still only words. can we come to grips with practical measures that will eliminate, or at least drastically reduce, the terrorist menace?

A.: There are no quick fixes or silver bullets. Any country that doesn't implement a solemn global treaty will face sanctions imposed by the Security Council. No sympathy and no exceptions.

Q.: What motives lie behind the kind of all-consuming hatred of the US demonstrated by such acts of barbarism?

A.: The feeling of injustice—and the root cause—is the Middle Eastern crisis. Muslims everywhere see America giving arms to the Israelis to kill Muslims, and America not putting any conditions on the arms it gives free to Israel. Muslims see the media taking the side of Israel whatever it does. Public opinion is seething against America which continues to support Israel irrespective of Sharon's policies that are designed to prevent the Palestinians from having their own state. Go to all the so-called moderate states in the region, from Jordan to Saudi Arabia, Kuwait, Qatar and Oman. Their leaders have told me that their streets are on the verge of boiling over.

Q.: So what is to be done in the immediate future?

A.: Both sides in the Palestinians-Israeli crisis should start implementing the US–sponsored Mitchell report [a Middle East

Egyptian president Hosni Mubarak waves to a crowd in Cairo. Mubarak strongly advised all nations of the world to sign a treaty to combat terrorism.

peace proposal], gradually but quickly, withdrawing Israeli tanks and troops from the occupied Palestinian territories. The increasingly desperate Palestinians are encircled. They cannot send their children to school. They cannot feed them. They cannot send them to hospital. They cannot earn a living. They cannot ... cannot ... cannot. So to recruit suicide bombers in such dire circumstances is not difficult.

Q.: Specifically, what should the US do to defuse the situation?

A.: The US must abandon its posture of diplomatic neglect that has led us to this impasse, and get [Israeli Prime Minister Ariel] Sharon to implement the Mitchell report with no further equivocation.

Q.: How does one use military muscle to combat the international terror network?

A.: First you need genuine real-time intelligence sharing—for example, between the Pakistani service and US agencies. They know a lot of critically important things. Secondly, you should bear in mind that spectacular precision bombing and Tomahawk missile attacks make nice headlines but are counterproductive. We need special forces to go in and kill the snake's head, not its tail, and then retreat.

Q.: You mean US special forces?

A.: No. From other countries. American forces would be seen in the Muslim world as evidence supporting the worst paranoid suspicions of the fundamentalist extremists.

Some countries are much better suited than the US for such operations.

Q.: But who would get the job of clearing out such (terrorist) groups as Hamas, Islamic Jihad, Hizbollah and other extremist groups that supply and train Kamikaze human bombs?

A.: (Dismissive wave of the hand). They are nothing, small fry on the world stage. As soon as the Palestinians get a viable independent state with all of East Jerusalem as their capital, you will see them fade away.

Q.: And what about countries like Libya and Iran that also harbor terrorist training camps?

A.: In Libya, I can assure you they are all gone and that Colonel Moammar Gaddhafi considers fundamentalist extremism as much of a threat as we do. As for Iran, I don't know.

Q.: Iraqi TV hailed the world's most devastating terrorist attack as "the operation of the century."

A.: Iraq is a special case.

Q.: But you can't dismiss the possibility that one of Iraq's intelligence services, Iran's revolutionary guards, Hizbollah and so forth bring aid and succor to the transnational network? US and British fighter bombers have spent the best part of 10 years bombing Iraqi anti-aircraft facilities. Wouldn't (Iraqi President) Saddam Hussein be interested in cooperating with bin Laden's network to get back at the US, his arch enemy?

A.: I don't think Iraq was involved. (Saddam) has no wish to unleash the wrath of the US.

Q.: So by process of elimination, you, too, have focused on Osama Bin Laden's al Qaida (the base) terrorist network. What do your intelligence services know about him?

A.: That he is very wealthy and spreads his money around Afghanistan.

Q.: The best estimates are that he has now run through his original family inheritance of some $200 million, and that's why the Taliban regime now regard him as more of a nuisance than an asset.

A.: Don't you believe it. He's worth at least one or two billion dollars.

Q.: How did his terrorist kitty [fortune] grow so large?

A.: The opium trade. But don't forget that Bin Laden's organization was America's creation after the Soviets invaded Afghanistan in late 1979—along with the recruitment of Afghan Arabs from all the Arab countries. After the Soviets left Afghanistan in 1989, America lost interest in Afghanistan and abandoned the Afghan Arabs. I think we know the rest of the story.

Excerpted from "Mubarak Gives Interview to UPI," by Arnaud de Borchgrave, United Press International, September 18, 2001. Copyright © 2001 by United Press International. Reprinted with permission.

Chapter Four

Who Is to Blame?

As rescue and recovery efforts got under way in New York, Washington. D.C., and Pennsylvania, governments and people around the world began assigning blame for the September 11, 2001, attacks to a terrorist leader named Osama bin Laden. Bin Laden, a Saudi Arabian exile living in Afghanistan, had been an opponent of the United States and its governmental policies for years. He had long condemned America and, the U.S. government suspected, had attacked two U. S. embassies and a U.S. Navy ship before.

As the United States pointed the finger at bin Laden, however, he pointed back. Initially denying responsibility, he claimed that the United States had brought the September 11 attacks on itself. He implied that America was bent on destroying the Muslim world and argued that, by supporting the country of Israel and by valuing political philoso-

phies that directly contradicted the teachings of Islam, the U.S. government and the citizens who supported that government, not the terrorists, were at fault.

He was not alone. Leaders in Iraq and Afghanistan agreed. Iraqi leader Saddam Hussein, for example, argued that American involvement in Middle Eastern politics had led to enormous resentment of the United States in the Arab world; the September 11 attacks, then, were justified retaliation for American interference. Likewise, Mohammad Omar, the head of Afghanistan's ruling Taliban government, refused to turn bin Laden over to the American government after the attacks, saying that to do so would violate Islamic tradition.

Middle Eastern leaders were not the only ones who claimed that America had brought the attacks on itself. At home, discussions about blame abounded. Although

Never mind

Reset

Irrelevant

they later retracted their statements, fundamentalist Christian ministers Jerry Falwell and Pat Robertson also initially took the stance that the United States was at fault. Falwell and Robertson said it was an absence of God in American households, schools, and government that led to the September 11 attacks.

Although there is little agreement among extremists, most Americans and world leaders take a simpler approach. They blame the terrorists themselves, holding the men who hijacked the planes and the people who financed and trained them responsible. Most consider the collapse of the World Trade Center and the plane crashes at the Pentagon and in Pennsylvania acts of war perpetrated by men who wanted nothing less than to destroy the Western world.

America Created the Evil Which Attacked It

In late September 2001, Mohammad Omar, the Taliban's leader, gave a twelve-minute interview to Voice of America, a publicly funded American radio station. During the interview, Omar says that the Taliban will continue to support Osama bin Laden and will not turn him over to the U.S. government.

Voice of America interviewer: Why don't you expel Osama bin Laden?

Taliban soldiers sit on top of a tank in Kandahar, Afghanistan.

Omar: This is not an issue of Osama bin Laden. It is an issue of Islam. Islam's prestige is at stake. So is Afghanistan's tradition.

VOA: Do you know that the US has announced a war on terrorism?

Omar: I am considering two promises. One is the promise of God, the other is that of Bush. The promise of God is that my land is vast. If you start a journey on God's path, you can reside anywhere on this earth and will be protected. . . . The promise of Bush is that there is no place on earth where you can hide that I cannot find you. We will see which one of these two promises is fulfilled.

VOA: But aren't you afraid for the people, yourself, the Taliban, your country?

Omar: Almighty God . . . is helping the believers and the Muslims. God says he will never be satisfied with the infidels. In terms of worldly affairs, America is very strong. Even if it were twice as strong or twice that, it could not be strong enough to defeat us. We are confident that no one can harm us if God is with us.

VOA: You are telling me you are not concerned, but Afghans all over the world are concerned.

Omar: We are also concerned. Great issues lie ahead. But we depend on God's mercy. Consider our point of view: if we give Osama away today, Muslims who are now pleading to give him up would then be reviling us for giving him up. . . . Everyone is afraid of America and wants to please it. But Americans will not be able to prevent such acts like the one that has just occurred because America has taken Islam hostage. If you look at Islamic countries, the people are

in despair. They are complaining that Islam is gone. But people remain firm in their Islamic beliefs. In their pain and frustration, some of them commit suicide acts. They feel they have nothing to lose.

VOA: What do you mean by saying America has taken the Islamic world hostage?

Omar: America controls the governments of the Islamic countries. The people ask to follow Islam, but the governments do not listen because they are in the grip of the United States. If someone follows the path of Islam, the government arrests him, tortures him or kills him. This is the doing of America. If it stops supporting those governments and lets the people deal with them, then such things won't happen. America has created the evil that is attacking it. The evil will not disappear even if I die and Osama dies and others die. The US should step back and review its policy. It should stop trying to impose its empire on the rest of the world, especially on Islamic countries.

VOA: So you won't give Osama bin Laden up?

Omar: No. We cannot do that. If we did, it means we are not Muslims . . . that Islam is finished. If we were afraid of attack, we could have surrendered him the last time we were threatened and attacked. So America can hit us again, and this time we don't even have a friend.

VOA: If you fight America with all your might—can the Taliban do that? Won't America beat you and won't your people suffer even more?

Omar: I'm very confident that it won't turn out this way. Please note this: there is nothing more we can do except depend on almighty God. If a person does, then he is assured that the Almighty will help him, have mercy on him and he will succeed.

Excerpted from "Mullah Omar–In His Own Words," by Mohammad Omar, interviewed by Voice of America, *The Guardian*, September 26, 2001.

America Deserves This Humiliation

Although the United States and other Western countries held terrorist leader Osama bin Laden responsible for the September 11 attacks, bin Laden claimed America had brought them on itself. In this excerpt, taken from a transcript of a videotaped recording, bin Laden explains and accuses the United States of hypocrisy.

I bear witness that there is no God but Allah and that Muhammad is his messenger.

There is America, hit by God in one of its softest spots. Its greatest buildings were destroyed, thank God for that. There is America, full of fear from its north to its south, from its west to its east. Thank God for that.

What America is tasting now is something insignificant compared to what we have tasted for scores of years. Our nation [the Islamic world] has been tasting this humiliation and this degradation for more than 80 years. Its sons are killed, its blood is shed, its sanctuaries are attacked, and no one hears and no one heeds.

When God blessed one of the groups of Islam, vanguards of Islam, they destroyed America. I pray to God to elevate their status and bless them.

Osama bin Laden is said to be the mastermind behind the September 11 attacks.

Millions of innocent children are being killed as I speak. They are being killed in Iraq without committing any sins, and we don't hear condemnation or a *fatwa* [religious decree] from the rulers. In these days, Israeli tanks infest Palestine—in Jenin, Ramallah, Rafah, Beit Jala and other places in the land of Islam—and we don't hear anyone raising his voice or moving a limb.

When the sword comes down [on America], after 80 years, hypocrisy rears its ugly head. They deplore and they lament for those killers, who have abused the blood, honor and sanctuaries of Muslims. The least that can be said about those people is that they are debauched. They have followed injustice. They supported the butcher over the victim, the oppressor over the innocent child. May God show them his wrath and give them what they deserve.

I say that the situation is clear and obvious. After this event, after the senior officials have spoken in America, starting with the head of infidels worldwide, Bush, and those with him. They have come out in force with their men and have turned even the countries that belong to Islam to this treachery, and they want to wag their tail at God, to fight Islam, to suppress people in the name of terrorism.

When people at the ends of the earth, Japan, were killed by their hundreds of thousands, young and old, it was not considered a war crime, it is something that has justification. Millions of children in Iraq is something that has justification. But when they lose dozens of people in Nairobi and Dar es Salaam [capitals of Kenya and Tanzania, where U.S. embassies were bombed in 1998], Iraq was struck and Afghanistan was struck. Hypocrisy stood in force behind the head of infidels worldwide, behind the cowards of this age, America and those who are with it.

These events have divided the whole world into two sides—the side of believers and the side of infidels. May God keep you away from them. Every Muslim has to rush to make his religion victorious. The winds of faith have come. The winds of change have come to eradicate oppression from the island of Muhammad, peace be upon him.

To America, I say only a few words to it and its people. I swear by God, who has elevated the skies without pillars, neither America nor the people who live in it will dream of security before we live it in Palestine, and not before all the infidel armies leave the land of Muhammad, peace be upon him.

God is great, may pride be with Islam. May peace and God's mercy be upon you.

Osama bin Laden, "Hypocrisy Rears Its Ugly Head," *Washington Post*, October 8, 2001, p. A12.

 ## Why America Was Attacked

In early October 2001, Saddam Hussein, the president and military leader of Iraq, responded to American criticism that his response to the September 11, 2001, terrorist attacks was callous and unsympathetic. In the excerpt below, Hussein explains that even though Muslims are against fanaticism of all kinds, American intervention in the Middle East has created resentment in the Arab world. Further, he argues, it is reasonable to expect Muslims to fight to oust Christians and Jews (in Israel and other areas of the Middle East) from Islam's holy lands and territories. In addition, Hussein claims that the United States refused to furnish proof showing who was responsible for the September 11 attacks. Thus, Hussein reasons, Americans should not expect sympathy from him or the Iraqi people for the victims' deaths.

The people of Iraq are against all kinds of fanaticism, whether based on religion, nationality or race. They are against the use of fanaticism as a cover for harming people whom God does not accept to harm. They call for love between the peoples and nations of the world. Nevertheless, we do not believe in love on one side only.

Iraq has been harmed severely by the fanaticism of others, including America. It was also severely harmed by terrorism. Maybe you don't know that many of the members of our leadership were victims of terrorism and terrorists. Some of them escaped death, by the will of God, after being injured or missed by the terrorists, in addition to the pain inflicted to our people.

Do you know brother, that your administration's reaction to that, was one of encouraging it and rejoicing? Do you know that your administration has been encouraging terrorism against us for the past eleven years, calling to overthrow us by force, allocating special funds to do so, and boasting about not fearing God, as it publicly announces that on TV screens, because Iraq does not have the same destructive force and armament of America? The Palestinians, whose right to resist the occupation forces are guaranteed by the international law, promulgated [declared] by America and the other big powers, are considered terrorists because they resist the Zionist [Israeli] occupation of their territories, and holy places.

Tell me, brother, if the Vatican is occupied by Arabs, or non-Arab Muslims, wouldn't its people fight the occupying forces? Wouldn't the English people fight for the Westminster cathedral? Or wouldn't the French people , defend Notre dame? I say they must fight for them! Why, then, are your armies occupying Mecca and the land of our Prophet? Why

are you occupying the regional waters in the Arab Gulf, in addition to territories in its countries? Why is your ally, the Zionist entity, occupying our holy places, and territories, in Palestine, by using your arms, and financial, political, media, and moral support? And, why are your administration killing people, including children in Iraq, Afghanistan, and in Palestine now, just as it did, before that, in Lebanon, Sudan, Somalia and Libya, and the list of Arabs and Muslims to be killed is long?!

I know that Arabs are far from being fanatic. Do you know why? Because, God, the Almighty, assigned them with the mission of delivering the messages of all religions to humanity, and not to Arabs alone. They have fulfilled their mission, so that all Christians are now indebted to Arabs for guiding them to Faith, which God wanted them to have when, He made it possible for them to reach you, or for you to reach them, so that you know what they believe in, and be affected by it.

I know that Arabs, in general, do not adopt fanatic stances against any people for religious reasons. But, can anyone guarantee that one fanaticism does not create another? Can anyone guarantee that the death toll and killing, inflicted upon Arabs and Muslims by the American armies, would not lead to a counter-reaction, whether that reaction is well guided, or is a random one, that pleases no one except those who carry it out?

These words are general rules and principles, although I still do not know who is behind what happened to the towers on September 11, 2001. Your government did not help me, or anyone else, by showing, or communicating the information it possesses, so that we can elaborate an opinion, if it needed to know the opinion of those whose people it daily attacks with bombs, starves to death, and deprives from the right to live, construct, and deploy their creativity.

Our law, which is borne of our religion and heritage, and of our reasoning which is thousands of years deep, stipulates: "the Plaintiff should present evidence and the defendant should take an oath." But the plaintiff, which is your administration did not present any evidence so far. Nevertheless, it accused the people it accused, without showing us, or anyone else, any evidence, except for Blair and the ruler of Palestine, as they both said. The people accused have not pleaded guilty.

Anyhow, I don't think that your administration deserves the condolences of Iraqis, except if it presents its condolences to the Iraqi people for the one million and a half Iraqis it killed, and apologizes to them, for the crimes it committed against them.

Excerpted from "A Letter from President Saddam Hussein to an American Citizen," by Saddam Hussein, www.ururlink.net, October 18, 2001.

 ## Terrorists Must Not Be Appeased

After the attacks of September 11, 2001, some commentators wrote that they believed some U.S. policies were partially responsible for the attacks. Jonathan Alter, a writer for Newsweek magazine, disagrees with these views. In this October 2001 article, he concedes that some American policies may have

infuriated Osama bin Laden, the reputed organizer of the attacks, but says that the attacks themselves were unjustified and evil. Citing the examples of World War II and Adolf Hitler, Alter concludes that appeasing terrorists will only encourage them to strike again.

After we attack the Taliban and the terrorists strike us again, you know what's going to happen. A big old-fashioned peace movement will emerge that blames the United States for whatever further destruction is inflicted. We'll be told that we "prompted" or "provoked" the gas attack, football-stadium bombing, assassination attempt, whatever. How do I know? Because a sizable chunk of what passes for the left is already knee-deep in ignorant and dangerous appeasement of the terrorism of Sept. 11. While moderate liberals (and even [liberal columnist] Christopher Hitchens) seem to get who the bad guys are, some of their brethren farther left—especially on college campuses—are unforgivably out to lunch.

Like President Bush and the vast majority of the country, I'm for a targeted war that tries hard to avoid civilian casualties, Islamic blowback and other unintended consequences. And I'll defend forever the right of anyone to say any stupid thing without being fired or hassled by the authorities. But some of what's being said can truly try one's patience, and I'm not just talking about Jerry Falwell and Pat Robertson's "Blame Homosexuality First" approach to explaining the attack.

The only thing worse than a silly politician analyzing art is a silly artist analyzing

A symbol of the U.S. presence in the Middle East, an American flag flies high above a U.S. military vehicle in Saudi Arabia.

politics. The New Republic's "Idiocy Watch," which is cataloging the fatuities [foolishness], is full of the musings of novelists. Bestselling writer Barbara Kingsolver, confused by the patriotism around her, asked in the San Francisco Chronicle whether the "flag stands for intimidation, censorship, violence, bigotry, sexism, homophobia, and shoving the Constitution through a paper shredder? Whom are we calling terrorists here?"

This mindless moral equivalency is the nub of what lefties mean when they talk about "the chickens coming home to roost," or "reaping what you sow." Talk about ironic: the same people always urging us to not blame the victim in rape cases are now saying Uncle Sam wore a short skirt and asked

for it. A haughty [essayist and novelist] Susan Sontag made it sound as if we were the ones being thickheaded for not seeing that Sept. 11 was a perfectly understandable response to years of American policy.

Obviously, some policies—like the United States' stationing troops in Saudi Arabia—have contributed to Osama bin Laden's rage. But there's a big difference between understanding Islam and the history of the region, which we need much more of, and understanding evil, which is not just offensive but impossible.

Sad to say, the line between explaining terrorism and rationalizing it has been repeatedly breached by a shallow left stuck in a deep anti-American rut. For certain (fortunately powerless) tenured radicals and antiwar vets, this post-Vietnam reflex seems as comfortable as an old sandal.

While most Americans view history through a "Greatest Generation" World War II prism, this remnant remembers how wrong that analogy was for Vietnam. The left was on target then: for years the United States refused to negotiate much with the communists out of a misplaced fear of seeming to be [early World War II British prime minister] Neville Chamberlain-style appeasers.

But history moves on, even for aging ideologues [idealists] heavily invested in the past. "National security" is not a government cover story anymore, but a genuine problem. The terrorists we're looking for aren't pathetic little pamphleteers, like the American communists targeted in the Red Scare. Reactionary left-wingers are still so busy thinking the CIA is malevolent [evil] that they forget to notice it's incompetent; so busy nursing stale resentments that they forget to notice someone is trying to kill them.

"The causal business is really pernicious [deadly]," says Peter Awn, a professor of Islamic religion at Columbia who says it results from ignorance of the complexities of the region. "People are going back to the one area they know something about—the Israeli-Palestinian struggle—and that's a shame. It shows their ability to understand the rest of the Islamic world is minimal."

The trick is to learn some lessons from the past without implying that we had it coming. We've done that before. After World War II our leaders saw that the punitive Versailles peace treaty following World War I had helped pave the way for Hitler. So we tried the generous Marshall Plan instead and it worked. But that came later. Only a fool would have given credence to Hitler's grievances, however legitimate a few of them were, while we were fighting him.

And none but a fool would say, as the novelist Alice Walker did in *The Village Voice*, that "the only punishment that works is love." We've tried turning the other cheek. After the 1993 World Trade Center bombing we held our fire and treated the attack as a law-enforcement matter. The terrorists struck again anyway. This time the Munich analogy is right: appeasement is doomed.

America Firsters grasped this point after Pearl Harbor and the isolationists ran off to enlist. So why can't Blame America Firsters grasp it now? Al Qaeda was planning its attack at exactly the time the United States was offering a Mideast peace deal favorable to the Palestinians. Nothing from us would have satisfied the fanatics, and nothing ever will. Peace won't be with you, brother. It's kill or be killed.

Jonathan Alter, "Blame America at Your Peril," *Newsweek*, October 15, 2001, p 41.

 ## God Has Withdrawn His Protection from America

Jerry Falwell and Pat Robertson are conservative Christian ministers. Robertson, a former Republican presidential candidate, has his own television show, The 700 Club. *Shortly after the terrorist attacks, his guest on the show was Jerry Falwell, and the two discussed the state of America following the September 11 attacks. Part of Falwell's statement, in which he placed blame for the*

attacks with the ACLU, abortion rights advocates, and feminists, among others, caused an uproar among Americans of all political persuasions. He later apologized for his comments, claiming that they were taken out of context and that he "misspoke."

Pat Robertson's Comments Preceding the Falwell Interview:

PAT ROBERTSON: And we have thought that we're invulnerable. And we have been so concerned about money. We have been so concerned about material things. The interests of people are on their health and their finances, and on their pleasures and on their sexuality, and while this is going on while we're self-absorbed and the churches as well as in the population, we have allowed rampant pornography on the internet. We have allowed rampant secularism and occult, etc. to be broadcast on television. We have permitted somewhere in the neighborhood of 35 to 40 million unborn babies to be slaughtered in our society. We have a court that has essentially stuck its finger in God's eye and said we're going to legislate you out of the schools. We're going to take your commandments from off the courthouse steps in various states. We're not going to let little children read the commandments of God. We're not going to let the Bible be read, no prayer in our schools. We have insulted God at the highest levels of our government. And, then we say 'why does this happen?'

Well, why it's happening is that God Almighty is lifting his protection from us. And once that protection is gone, we all are vulnerable because we're a free society, and

we're vulnerable. We lay naked before these terrorists who have infiltrated our country. There's probably tens of thousands of them in America right now. They've been raising money. They've been preaching their hate and overseas they have been spewing out venom against the United States for years. All over the Arab world, there is venom being poured out into people's ears and minds against America. And, the only thing that's going to sustain us is the umbrella power of the Almighty God....

The Interview with Jerry Falwell:

PAT ROBERTSON: Well after Tuesday's attacks, many Americans are struggling with grief, fear and unanswered questions. How should Christians respond to this crisis? Well joining us now with some answers is a dear friend of ours, the Pastor of the Thomas Road Baptist Church and Liberty University, the head and founder of that, Dr. Jerry Falwell. Jerry, it's a delight to have you with us today.

JERRY FALWELL: Thanks, Pat.

PAT ROBERTSON: Listen. What are you telling the church? You called your church together. What was your response at Thomas Road to this tragedy?

JERRY FALWELL: Well, as the world knows, the tragedy hit on Tuesday morning, and at 2:00 in the afternoon, we gathered 7,000 Liberty University students, faculty, local people together, and we used the verse that I heard you use a moment ago, Chronicles II, 7:14, that God wanted us to humble ourselves and seek his face. And there's not much we can do in the Church but what we're supposed to do, and that is pray. Pray for the President that God will give him wisdom, keep bad advisors from him, bring good ones to him, praying for the families of the victims, praying for America. And, you know this thing is not a great deal different than what I remember and you Pat. We're about the same age. December 7, 1941, when we entered the war against Japan, Germany, Italy. Hitler's goal was to destroy the Jews among other things, and conquer the world. And, these Islamic fundamentalists, these radical terrorists, these Middle Eastern monsters are committed to destroying the Jewish nation, driving her into the Mediterranean, conquering the world. And, we are the great Satan. We are the ultimate goal. I talked this morning with Tom Rose publisher of the *Jerusalem Post*, and orthodox Jew, and he said, "Now America knows in a horrible way what Israel's been facing for 53 years at the hand of Arafat and other terrorists and radicals and barbarians."

PAT ROBERTSON: Jerry, I know that you shared several 40 day fasts for revival in America. We here at CBN [Christian Broadcasting Network] had a couple of 40 day fasts during the Lenten season, and Bill Bright, I don't know, eight or nine. Do you think that this is going to be the trigger of revival, a real revival in the Church where we truly turn back to God with all our heart?

JERRY FALWELL: It could be. I've never sensed a togetherness, a burden, a broken heart as I do in the Church today, and just 48 hours, I gave away a booklet I wrote 10 years ago. I gave it away last night on the

Biblical position on fasting and prayer because I do believe that that is what we've got to do now—fast and pray. And I agree totally with you that the Lord has protected us so wonderfully these 225 years. And since 1812, this is the first time that we've been attacked on our soil, first time, and by far the worst results. And I fear, as Donald Rumsfeld, the Secretary of Defense said yesterday, that this is only the beginning. And with biological warfare available to these monsters; the Husseins, the Bin Ladens, the Arafats, what we saw on Tuesday, as terrible as it is, could be miniscule if, in fact, if in fact God continues to lift the curtain and allow the enemies of America to give us probably what we deserve.

PAT ROBERTSON: Jerry, that's my feeling. I think we've just seen the antechamber to terror. We haven't even begun to see what they can do to the major population.

JERRY FALWELL: The ACLU's [American Civil Liberties Union] got to take a lot of blame for this.

PAT ROBERTSON: Well, yes.

JERRY FALWELL: And, I know that I'll hear from them for this. But, throwing God out successfully with the help of the federal court system, throwing God out of the public square, out of the schools. The abortionists have got to bear some burden for this because God will not be mocked. And when we destroy 40 million little innocent babies, we make God mad. I really believe that the pagans, and the abortionists, and the feminists, and the gays and the lesbians who are actively trying to make that an alternative lifestyle, the ACLU, People For the American

Way, all of them who have tried to secularize America. I point the finger in their face and say 'you helped this happen.'

PAT ROBERTSON: Well, I totally concur, and the problem is we have adopted that agenda at the highest levels of our government. And so we're responsible as a free society for what the top people do. And, the top people, of course, is the court system.

JERRY FALWELL: Amen. Pat, did you notice yesterday? The ACLU, and all the Christ-haters, the People For the American Way, NOW, etc. were totally disregarded by the Democrats and the Republicans in both houses of Congress as they went out on the steps and called out on to God in prayer and sang 'God Bless America' and said 'let the ACLU be hanged.' In other words, when the nation is on its knees, the only normal and natural and spiritual thing to do is what we ought to be doing all the time—calling upon God.

PAT ROBERTSON: Amen. I wanted to ask you the reaction. I know that you had a

In an interview with Pat Robertson (*left*), Jerry Falwell (*right*) discussed his views on who is to blame for terrorism in the United States.

major prayer meeting last night, and I know your people assembled, just a large gathering at your church. What was the mood of the people? What did they say and what did you sense with your congregation?

JERRY FALWELL: A brokenness that I have not seen. I've been their pastor 45 years, 30 years Chancellor at Liberty. We had 7,000 gather yesterday in the Vines Center and filled the Church last night. I sensed a brokenness, tears. People were sobbing at the altar. And, they have no shame about it. It was the kind of brokenness that no one could conjure, only God could bring upon us. And, that is to me the most optimistic thing that I see today as I look across America. And every city, I called a friend in Springfield yesterday. He said at least a hundred churches, Springfield, MO [Missouri], at least a hundred churches have special prayer meetings for America today and tonight. And, that's happening by the thousands all over America. This could be, if we will fast and pray, this could be God's call to revival.

PAT ROBERTSON: Well, I believe it. And I think the people, the Bible says render your hearts and not your garments, and people begin to render their hearts and they weep before the Lord, and they really get serious with God, God will hear and answer. We'll see revival. I am thrilled to hear that about your church because it's happening all over.

JERRY FALWELL: It's everywhere.

PAT ROBERTSON: Yes.

JERRY FALWELL: In the most unlikely of places. The general manager at the ABC affiliate in our area called me this morning and said "we're going to ask for all the churches, all the people of faith to join us at the D-Day Memorial over in Bedford at 2:00, Sunday." And, Randy Smith is his name, the general manager, and he is calling central Virginia to healing through prayer and I suspect there will be thousands there.

PAT ROBERTSON: Jerry, this is so encouraging, and I thank God for your stand. We just love you and praise God for you. Liberty is a great institution and I congratulate you for that wonderful student body, and your church. And, thank-you my dear friend for being with us.

JERRY FALWELL: God bless you brother. Let's stand together.

PAT ROBERTSON: Amen.

 ## Allah Be Praised!

The following selection is an excerpt from a videotape on which Osama bin Laden talks about the attacks on the World Trade Center and the Pentagon. On the tape, he is surrounded by his supporters, including an unidentified Saudi Arabian sheik (Shaykh), and is attending an informal dinner in Kandahar, Afghanistan, in mid-November 2001. The transcipt is choppy because the videotape begins with the second half of the dinner meeting and ends with the first half. In this excerpt, the sheik praises bin Laden for the success of the September 11, 2001, attacks and tells him that Islam remains strong following the attacks; it has even gained many new converts. Further, bin Laden claims to have known about the attacks days before

A videotape shows Osama bin Laden (*left*) at a meeting in Kandahar in November 2001. On the tape, he and a supporter (*right*) are heard discussing the September 11 attacks.

they occurred, despite previous statements denying personal responsibility.

SHAYKH: (*Describing the trip to the meeting*) They smuggled us and then I thought that we would be in different caves inside the mountains so I was surprised at the guest house and that it is very clean and comfortable. Thanks be to Allah, we also learned that this location is safe, by Allah's blessings. The place is clean and we are very comfortable.

[Osama bin Laden]: When people see a strong horse and a weak horse, by nature, they will like the strong horse. This is only one goal; those who want people to worship the lord of the people, without following that doctrine, will be following the doctrine of Muhammad, peace be upon him.

(*bin Laden quotes several short and incomplete Hadith verses [reports of the sayings of the prophet Muhammad], as follows*):

"I was ordered to fight the people until they say there is no god but Allah, and his prophet Muhammad."

"Some people may ask: why do you want to fight us?"

"There is an association between those who say: I believe in one god and Muhammad is his prophet, and those who don't (. . . *inaudible.* . .)

"Those who do not follow the true fiqh [legal rulings by muslim scholars on Islamic law]. The fiqh of Muhammad, the real fiqh. They are just accepting what is being said at face value."

bin Laden: Those youth who conducted the operations [the terrorist attacks] did not accept any fiqh in the popular terms, but they accepted the fiqh that the prophet Muhammad brought. Those young men (...*inaudible*...) said in deeds, in New York and Washington, speeches that overshadowed all other speeches made everywhere else in the world. The speeches are understood by both Arabs and non-Arabs—even by Chinese. It is above all the media said. Some of them said that in Holland, at one of the centers, the number of people who accepted Islam during the days that followed the operations were more than the people who accepted Islam in the last eleven years. I heard someone on Islamic radio who owns a school in America say: "We don't have time to keep up with the demands of those who are asking about Islamic books to learn about Islam." This event made people think (*about true Islam*) which benefited Islam greatly.

SHAYKH: Hundreds of people used to doubt you and few only would follow you until this huge event happened. Now hundreds of people are coming out to join you. I remember a vision by Shaykh Salih Al-((Shuaybi)). He said: "There will be a great hit and people will go out by hundreds to Afghanistan." I asked him (*Salih*): "To Afghanistan?" He replied, "Yes." According to him, the only ones who stay behind will be the mentally impotent and the liars (*hypocrites*). I remembered his saying that hundreds of people will go out to Afghanistan. He had this vision a year ago. This event discriminated between the different types of followers.

bin Laden: (...*Inaudible*...) we calculated in advance the number of casualties from the enemy, who would be killed based on the position of the tower. We calculated that the floors that would be hit would be three or four floors. I was the most optimistic of them all. (...*Inaudible*...) due to my experience in this field, I was thinking that the fire from the gas in the plane would melt the iron structure of the building and collapse the area where the plane hit and all the floors above it only. This is all that we had hoped for.

SHAYKH: Allah be praised.

bin Laden: We were at (...*Inaudible*...) when the event took place. We had notification since the previous Thursday that the event would take place that day. We had finished our work that day and had the radio on. It was 5:30 P.M. our time. I was sitting with Dr. Ahmad Abu-al-((Khair)). Immediately, we heard the news that a plane had hit the World Trade Center. We turned the radio station to the news from Washington. The news continued and no mention of the attack until the end. At the end of the newscast, they reported that a plane just hit the World Trade Center.

SHAYKH: Allah be praised.

bin Laden: After a little while, they announced that another plane had hit the World Trade Center. The brothers who heard the news were overjoyed by it.

SHAYKH: I listened to the news and I was sitting. We didn't ... we were not thinking about anything, and all of a sudden, Allah willing, we were talking about how come we

Palestinians cheer in the streets of Beirut after learning of the terrorist attacks on America.

didn't have anything, and all of a sudden the news came and everyone was overjoyed and everyone until the next day, in the morning, was talking about what was happening and we stayed until four o'clock, listening to the news every time a little bit different, everyone was very joyous and saying "Allah is great," "Allah is great," "We are thankful to Allah," "Praise Allah." And I was happy for the happiness of my brothers. That day the congratulations were coming on the phone non-stop. The mother was receiving phone calls continuously. Thank Allah. Allah is great, praise be to Allah.

(*Quoting the verse from the Quran*)

SHAYKH: "Fight them, Allah will torture them, with your hands, he will torture them. He will deceive them and he will give you victory. Allah will forgive the believers, he is knowledgeable about everything."

SHAYKH: No doubt it is a clear victory. Allah has bestowed on us . . . honor on us . . . and he will give us blessing and more victory during this holy month of Ramadan. And this is what everyone is hoping for. Thank Allah America came out of its caves. We hit her the first hit and the next one will hit her with the hands of the believers, the good believers, the strong believers. By Allah it is a great work. Allah prepares for you a great reward for this work. I'm sorry to speak in your presence, but it is just thoughts, just thoughts. By Allah, who there is no god but him. I live in happiness, happiness . . . I have not experienced, or felt, in a long time. . . .

Tape ends here. Second segment of bin Laden's visit, shows up at front of the tape . . .

SULAYMAN (ABU GUAITH): I was sitting with the Shaykh in a room, then I left to go to another room where there was a TV set. The TV broadcasted the big event. The scene was showing an Egyptian family sitting in their living room, they exploded with joy. Do you know when there is a soccer game and your team wins, it was the same expression of joy. There was a subtitle that read: "In revenge for the children of Al Aqsa', Usama Bin Ladin executes an operation against America." So I went back to the Shaykh (meaning bin Laden) who was sitting in a room with 50 to 60 people. I tried to tell him about what I saw, but he made gesture with his hands, meaning: "I know, I know . . ."

bin Laden: He did not know about the operation. Not everybody knew (. . . *Inaudible* . . .). Muhammad ((Atta)) from the Egyptian family (*meaning the Al Qa'ida Egyptian group*), was in charge of the group.

SHAYKH: A plane crashing into a tall building was out of anyone's imagination. This was a great job. He was one of the pious men in the organization. He became a martyr. Allah bless his soul.

SHAYKH (*Referring to dreams and visions*): The plane that he saw crashing into the building was seen before by more than one person. One of the good religious people has left everything and come here. He told me, "I saw a vision, I was in a huge plane, long and wide. I was carrying it on my shoulders and I walked from the road to the desert for half a kilometer. I was dragging the plane." I listened to him and I prayed to Allah to help him. Another person told me that last year he saw, but I didn't understand and I told him I don't understand. He said, "I saw people who left for jihad . . . and they found themselves in New York . . . in Washington and New York." I said, "What is this?" He told me the plane hit the building. That was last year. We haven't thought much about it. But, when the incidents happened he came to me and said, "Did you see . . . this is strange." I have another man . . . my god . . . he said and swore by Allah that his wife had seen the incident a week earlier. She saw the plane crashing into a building . . . that was unbelievable, my god.

bin Laden: The brothers, who conducted the operation, all they knew was that they have a martyrdom operation and we asked each of them to go to America but they didn't know anything about the operation, not even one letter. But they were trained and we did not reveal the operation to them until they are there and just before they boarded the planes.

bin Laden: (. . . *Inaudible* . . .) then he said: Those who were trained to fly didn't know the others. One group of people did not know the other group. (. . . *Inaudible* . . .) . . .

bin Laden: The difference between the first and the second plane hitting the towers was twenty minutes. And the difference between the first plane and the plane that hit the Pentagon was one hour.

SHAYKH: They (the Americans) were terrified thinking there was a coup.

Transcript of videotape of Osama bin Laden meeting with followers somewhere in Afghanistan, probably in mid-November 2001. Released by U.S. Department of Defense December 13, 2001. www.defenselink.mil/news/Dec2001/d20011213ubl.pdf.

Chapter Five

The War on Terrorism

L ess than one month after the September 11 attacks, the United States and its allies officially began their war on terrorism by initiating a bombing campaign in Afghanistan. Unofficially, however, the war had begun almost immediately. In the hours, days, and weeks after the first plane hit the World Trade Center, the United States military had begun patrolling American skies. National Guardsmen watched over airports. And armed air marshals, undercover law enforcement personnel, accompanied passengers on many domestic flights.

These early efforts gave way to a series of antiterrorism laws enacted by the president and U.S. Congress. The new laws gave FBI officials expanded authority to tap the phone lines and e-mail communications of people suspected of terrorism. They imposed harsh penalties on those convicted of

harboring or financing terrorists and allowed the U.S. government to detain and hold terrorism suspects for seven days without charging them with a crime.

Meanwhile, in the Middle East, the U.S. military was mobilizing for war. Air force, navy, and Marine pilots took positions on ships in the Arabian Sea. Soldiers prepared for combat. And then on October 7, 2001, U.S. warplanes bombed the first targets in Afghanistan. Initially, the targets included Taliban military positions—air fields, weapons' holds, and such. As the war progressed, the strikes specifically targeted bin Laden and his network of al-Qaeda terrorists, destroying training camps and caves where they were suspected to be hiding. With the help of the Northern Alliance, a group of Afghan rebels who had been fighting the Taliban since the mid-1990s, the war progressed quickly; by the end of the year, all major Taliban- and al-Qaeda-held cities had fallen to the Allies.

The war effort enjoyed much popular support. Having witnessed the destructive power of bin Laden and his followers, most Americans saw war as a justifiable response. There were those, however, who did not agree with the government's decisions. American civil liberties groups, in particular, argued that the new antiterrorism laws would infringe on individual rights. They worried that the laws would unfairly target legal immigrants and those who disagreed with the government's policies. Pacifists also criticized the war, arguing that avenging the victims' deaths with more violence was unjust.

Regardless, the war on terrorism continued. President Bush, his team of advisers, and leaders around the world maintained that it was indeed just, honorable, and necessary. Without it, they worried, the terrorist threat could not be eliminated.

Our Enemies: Osama bin Laden and Terrorism

A primary objective after the September 11 attacks was to discover who was behind them. In this excerpt of a speech given to a joint session of Congress on September 20, 2001, President George W. Bush identifies a terrorist network known as al-Qaeda and its leader, Osama bin Laden, as responsible for the attacks. Bush outlines America's demands to the Taliban government of Afghanistan, which harbored bin Laden, and reiterates the country's resolve to fight terrorism around the world.

Mr. Speaker, Mr. President Pro Tempore, members of Congress, and fellow Americans:

In the normal course of events, Presidents come to this chamber to report on the state of the Union. Tonight, no such report is needed. It has already been delivered by the American people.

We have seen it in the courage of passengers, who rushed terrorists to save others on the ground—passengers like an exceptional man named Todd Beamer. And would you please help me to welcome his wife, Lisa Beamer, here tonight.

We have seen the state of our Union in the endurance of rescuers, working past exhaustion. We have seen the unfurling of flags, the lighting of candles, the giving of blood, the saying of prayers—in English, Hebrew, and Arabic. We have seen the decency of a loving and giving people who have made the grief of strangers their own.

My fellow citizens, for the last nine days, the entire world has seen for itself the state of our Union—and it is strong.

Tonight we are a country awakened to danger and called to defend freedom. Our grief has turned to anger, and anger to resolution. Whether we bring our enemies to justice, or bring justice to our enemies, justice will be done.

I thank the Congress for its leadership at such an important time. All of America was touched on the evening of the tragedy to see Republicans and Democrats joined together on the steps of this Capitol, singing "God Bless America." And you did more than sing;

you acted, by delivering $40 billion to rebuild our communities and meet the needs of our military.

Speaker Hastert, Minority Leader Gephardt, Majority Leader Daschle and Senator Lott, I thank you for your friendship, for your leadership and for your service to our country.

And on behalf of the American people, I thank the world for its outpouring of support. America will never forget the sounds of our National Anthem playing at Buckingham Palace, on the streets of Paris, and at Berlin's Brandenburg Gate.

We will not forget South Korean children gathering to pray outside our embassy in Seoul, or the prayers of sympathy offered at a mosque in Cairo. We will not forget moments of silence and days of mourning in Australia and Africa and Latin America.

Nor will we forget the citizens of 80 other nations who died with our own: dozens of Pakistanis; more than 130 Israelis; more than 250 citizens of India; men and women from El Salvador, Iran, Mexico and Japan; and hundreds of British citizens. America has no truer friend than Great Britain. Once again, we are joined together in a great cause—so honored the British Prime Minister has crossed an ocean to show his unity of purpose with America. Thank you for coming, friend.

On September the 11th, enemies of freedom committed an act of war against our country. Americans have known wars—but for the past 136 years, they have been wars on foreign soil, except for one Sunday in 1941. Americans have known the casualties of war—but not at the center of a great city on a peaceful morning. Americans have known surprise attacks—but never before on thousands of civilians. All of this was brought upon us in a single day—and night fell on a different world, a world where freedom itself is under attack.

Americans have many questions tonight. Americans are asking: Who attacked our country? The evidence we have gathered all points to a collection of loosely affiliated terrorist organizations known as al Qaeda. They are the same murderers indicted for bombing American embassies in Tanzania and Kenya, and responsible for bombing the *USS Cole.*

Al Qaeda is to terror what the mafia is to crime. But its goal is not making money; its goal is remaking the world—and imposing its radical beliefs on people everywhere.

The terrorists practice a fringe form of Islamic extremism that has been rejected by Muslim scholars and the vast majority of Muslim clerics—a fringe movement that perverts the peaceful teachings of Islam. The terrorists' directive commands them to kill Christians and Jews, to kill all Americans, and make no distinction among military and civilians, including women and children.

This group and its leader—a person named Osama bin Laden—are linked to many other organizations in different countries, including the Egyptian Islamic Jihad and the Islamic Movement of Uzbekistan. There are thousands of these terrorists in more than 60 countries. They are recruited from their own nations and neighborhoods and brought to camps in places like Afghanistan, where they are trained in the tactics of terror. They are sent back to their homes or sent to hide in countries around the world to plot evil and destruction.

The leadership of al Qaeda has great influence in Afghanistan and supports the Taliban regime in controlling most of that country. In Afghanistan, we see al Qaeda's vision for the world.

Afghanistan's people have been brutalized—many are starving and many have fled.

Women are not allowed to attend school. You can be jailed for owning a television. Religion can be practiced only as their leaders dictate. A man can be jailed in Afghanistan if his beard is not long enough.

The United States respects the people of Afghanistan—after all, we are currently its largest source of humanitarian aid—but we condemn the Taliban regime. It is not only repressing its own people, it is threatening people everywhere by sponsoring and sheltering

Supporters of Osama bin Laden train in full gear at a camp in Afghanistan.

and supplying terrorists. By aiding and abetting murder, the Taliban regime is committing murder.

And tonight, the United States of America makes the following demands on the Taliban: Deliver to United States authorities all the leaders of al Qaeda who hide in your land. Release all foreign nationals, including American citizens, you have unjustly imprisoned. Protect foreign journalists, diplomats and aid workers in your country. Close immediately and permanently every terrorist training camp in Afghanistan, and hand over every terrorist, and every person in their support structure, to appropriate authorities. Give the United States full access to terrorist training camps, so we can make sure they are no longer operating.

These demands are not open to negotiation or discussion. The Taliban must act, and act immediately. They will hand over the terrorists, or they will share in their fate.

I also want to speak tonight directly to Muslims throughout the world. We respect your faith. It's practiced freely by many millions of Americans, and by millions more in countries that America counts as friends. Its teachings are good and peaceful, and those who commit evil in the name of Allah blaspheme the name of Allah. The terrorists are traitors to their own faith, trying, in effect, to hijack Islam itself. The enemy of America is not our many Muslim friends; it is not our many Arab friends. Our enemy is a radical network of terrorists, and every government that supports them.

Our war on terror begins with al Qaeda, but it does not end there. It will not end until every terrorist group of global reach has been found, stopped and defeated.

Americans are asking, why do they hate us? They hate what we see right here in this chamber—a democratically elected government. Their leaders are self-appointed. They hate our freedoms—our freedom of religion, our freedom of speech, our freedom to vote and assemble and disagree with each other.

They want to overthrow existing governments in many Muslim countries, such as Egypt, Saudi Arabia, and Jordan. They want to drive Israel out of the Middle East. They want to drive Christians and Jews out of vast regions of Asia and Africa.

These terrorists kill not merely to end lives, but to disrupt and end a way of life. With every atrocity, they hope that America grows fearful, retreating from the world and forsaking our friends. They stand against us, because we stand in their way.

We are not deceived by their pretenses to piety. We have seen their kind before. They are the heirs of all the murderous ideologies of the 20th century. By sacrificing human life to serve their radical visions—by abandoning every value except the will to power—they follow in the path of fascism, and Nazism, and totalitarianism. And they will follow that path all the way, to where it ends: in history's unmarked grave of discarded lies.

Americans are asking: How will we fight and win this war? We will direct every resource at our command—every means of diplomacy, every tool of intelligence, every instrument of law enforcement, every financial influence, and every necessary weapon of war—to the disruption and to the defeat of the global terror network.

This war will not be like the war against Iraq a decade ago, with a decisive liberation of territory and a swift conclusion. It will not look like the air war above Kosovo two years ago, where no ground troops were used and not a single American was lost in combat.

Our response involves far more than instant retaliation and isolated strikes. Americans should not expect one battle, but a lengthy campaign, unlike any other we have ever seen. It may include dramatic strikes, visible on TV, and covert operations, secret even in success. We will starve terrorists of funding, turn them one against another, drive them from place to place, until there is no refuge or no rest. And we will pursue nations that provide aid or safe haven to terrorism. Every nation, in every region, now has a decision to make. Either you are with us, or you are with the terrorists. From this day forward, any nation that continues to harbor or support terrorism will be regarded by the United States as a hostile regime.

Our nation has been put on notice: We are not immune from attack. We will take defensive measures against terrorism to protect Americans. Today, dozens of federal departments and agencies, as well as state and local governments, have responsibilities affecting homeland security. These efforts must be coordinated at the highest level. So tonight I announce the creation of a Cabinet-level position reporting directly to me—the Office of Homeland Security.

And tonight I also announce a distinguished American to lead this effort, to strengthen American security: a military veteran, an effective governor, a true patriot, a trusted friend—Pennsylvania's Tom Ridge. He will lead, oversee and coordinate a comprehensive national strategy to safeguard our country against terrorism, and respond to any attacks that may come.

These measures are essential. But the only way to defeat terrorism as a threat to our way of life is to stop it, eliminate it, and destroy it where it grows.

Many will be involved in this effort, from FBI agents to intelligence operatives to the reservists we have called to active duty. All deserve our thanks, and all have our prayers. And tonight, a few miles from the damaged Pentagon, I have a message for our military: Be ready. I've called the Armed Forces to alert, and there is a reason. The hour is coming when America will act, and you will make us proud.

This is not, however, just America's fight. And what is at stake is not just America's freedom. This is the world's fight. This is civilization's fight. This is the fight of all who believe in progress and pluralism, tolerance and freedom.

We ask every nation to join us. We will ask, and we will need, the help of police forces, intelligence services, and banking systems around the world. The United States is grateful that many nations and many international organizations have already responded—with sympathy and with support. Nations from Latin America, to Asia, to Africa, to Europe, to the Islamic world.

Perhaps the NATO Charter reflects best the attitude of the world: An attack on one is an attack on all.

The civilized world is rallying to America's side. They understand that if this terror goes unpunished, their own cities, their own citizens may be next. Terror, unanswered, can not only bring down buildings, it can threaten the stability of legitimate governments. And you know what—we're not going to allow it.

Americans are asking: What is expected of us? I ask you to live your lives, and hug your children. I know many citizens have fears tonight, and I ask you to be calm and resolute, even in the face of a continuing threat.

I ask you to uphold the values of America, and remember why so many have come here. We are in a fight for our principles, and our first responsibility is to live by them. No one should be singled out for unfair treatment or unkind words because of their ethnic background or religious faith.

I ask you to continue to support the victims of this tragedy with your contributions. Those who want to give can go to a central source of information, libertyunites.org, to find the names of groups providing direct help in New York, Pennsylvania, and Virginia.

The thousands of FBI agents who are now at work in this investigation may need your cooperation, and I ask you to give it.

I ask for your patience, with the delays and inconveniences that may accompany tighter security; and for your patience in what will be a long struggle.

I ask your continued participation and confidence in the American economy.

Terrorists attacked a symbol of American prosperity. They did not touch its source. America is successful because of the hard work, and creativity, and enterprise of our people. These were the true strengths of our economy before September 11th, and they are our strengths today.

And, finally, please continue praying for the victims of terror and their families, for those in uniform, and for our great country. Prayer has comforted us in sorrow, and will help strengthen us for the journey ahead.

Tonight I thank my fellow Americans for what you have already done and for what you will do. And ladies and gentlemen of the Congress, I thank you, their representatives, for what you have already done and for what we will do together.

Tonight, we face new and sudden national challenges. We will come together to improve air safety, to dramatically expand the number of air marshals on domestic flights, and take new measures to prevent hijacking. We will come together to promote stability and keep our airlines flying, with direct assistance during this emergency.

We will come together to give law enforcement the additional tools it needs to track down terror here at home. We will come together to strengthen our intelligence capabilities to know the plans of terrorists before they act, and find them before they strike.

We will come together to take active steps that strengthen America's economy, and put our people back to work.

Tonight we welcome two leaders who embody the extraordinary spirit of all New Yorkers: Governor George Pataki, and

Mayor Rudolph Guiliani. As a symbol of America's resolve, my administration will work with Congress, and these two leaders, to show the world that we will rebuild New York City.

After all that has just passed—all the lives taken, and all the possibilities and hopes that died with them—it is natural to wonder if America's future is one of fear. Some speak of an age of terror. I know there are struggles ahead, and dangers to face. But this country will define our times, not be defined by them. As long as the United States of America is determined and strong, this will not be an age of terror; this will be an age of liberty, here and across the world.

Great harm has been done to us. We have suffered great loss. And in our grief and anger we have found our mission and our moment. Freedom and fear are at war. The advance of human freedom—the great achievement of our time, and the great hope of every time—now depends on us. Our nation—this generation—will lift a dark threat of violence from our people and our future. We will rally the world to this cause by our efforts, by our courage. We will not tire, we will not falter, and we will not fail.

It is my hope that in the months and years ahead, life will return almost to normal. We'll go back to our lives and routines, and that is good. Even grief recedes with time and grace. But our resolve must not pass. Each of us will remember what happened that day, and to whom it happened. We'll remember the moment the news came— where we were and what we were doing. Some will remember an image of a fire, or a

story of rescue. Some will carry memories of a face and a voice gone forever.

And I will carry this: It is the police shield of a man named George Howard, who died at the World Trade Center trying to save others. It was given to me by his mom, Arlene, as a proud memorial to her son. This is my reminder of lives that ended, and a task that does not end.

I will not forget this wound to our country or those who inflicted it. I will not yield; I will not rest; I will not relent in waging this struggle for freedom and security for the American people.

The course of this conflict is not known, yet its outcome is certain. Freedom and fear, justice and cruelty, have always been at war, and we know that God is not neutral between them.

Fellow citizens, we'll meet violence with patient justice—assured of the rightness of our cause, and confident of the victories to come. In all that lies before us, may God grant us wisdom, and may He watch over the United States of America.

Excerpted from George W. Bush's "Address to a Joint Session of Congress and the American People," September 20, 2001.

 ## An Act of War

In this article Helle Bering, an editor at the Washington Times, *argues that crashing hijacked airplanes into American buildings is not a tragedy, but an act of war. Bering further contends that the United States must forcefully retaliate, she says, or expect more American deaths in the future.*

Could we stop calling this a "tragedy?" The hijacking of planes from American and United Airlines by terrorists, who crashed them into the two World Trade Center towers and the Pentagon, represent an act of war. It's that simple. Yesterday's [September 11, 2001] carnage may not have been preceded by a hand-delivered notice and a finely worded declaration of war, but such formalities are not the nature of warfare in the 21st century. Come to think of it, no formalities were observed at Pearl Harbor either, which caught the U.S. government equally unprepared. Yesterday was a "day of infamy" no less than Dec. 7, 1941.

Still, as in the war with Japan 60 years ago, it is not as though we have not been put on notice over the past decade. For years, Islamic terrorists have considered themselves at war with the United States and its ally Israel, whose vulnerability to suicide bombings ought to be especially appreciated by Americans today. What we felt here yesterday, from astonishment to helplessness to absolute outrage, is what the Israelis have to live with every single day.

Our recent experience with Islamic terrorism ought to have placed the country on high alert. The World Trade Center bombing of 1993 was a warning. So, too, was the bombing of two U.S. embassies in Africa in 1998. So was the bombing of the USS *Cole* in Yemen in October of last year.

Forces of darkness are indeed conspiring against us, people who act in ways that we consider neither rational nor intelligible. They do have a sick logic of their own, however. Saudi fundamentalist terrorist leader Osama bin Laden has been fingered as a prime suspect in the coordinated embassy bombings in Africa, and he has reportedly bragged about the attack on the USS *Cole*. Reports of an imminent and massive attack on the United States have apparently been around for the past several weeks.

So, it surely is not unfair to ask why the U.S. security services were asleep again. As an outraged [congressional] Rep. Curt Weldon fumed yesterday on CNN, "the first priority of the U.S. government is not education, it is not health care, it is the defense and protection of U.S. citizens." [Congressional] Rep. Dana Rohrabacher is very reasonably demanding accountability among high-level intelligence officials. An operation of this magnitude and level of precise coordination should have been picked up by the CIA or the FBI. Whether the reason is complacency, a lack of funding or a lack of human assets in countries that harbor and nourish terrorists, it is totally incomprehensible and unforgivable that the United States was caught off-guard again.

President Bush preserved calm during one of the worst days a U.S. president could have imagined. Calm is good. But if anything, one would have liked the president to have spoken more in anger than in sadness, which seemed to be his prevailing mode. "Make no mistake," Mr. Bush stated, "the United States will hunt down and punish those responsible for these cowardly acts." Acknowledging that "[t]he resolve of our great nation is being tested," Mr. Bush promised, "We will show the world that we will pass this test." He had better follow through on that. The actions of Mr. Bush— and of every country that wishes to be called a friend of the United States—will be carefully watched by the enemy. This is not a time to urge caution. We have to respond with massive retaliation or expect more American lives to be lost in the future.

Somewhat encouragingly, it seems that this is also the expectation felt abroad. Palestinian leader Yasser Arafat was among the first to deplore the action, looking severely shaken. Perhaps he could inform his people that their dancing in the streets of the West Bank and handing out candy in celebration does not exactly back up his regrets. Meanwhile, Islamic Jihad [a fundamentalist Islamic group] in Gaza issued a statement blaming U.S. Middle East policy, but renouncing any responsibility. Even the odious [hated] Taliban in Afghanistan held a press conference to let it be known that they didn't do it. Nor did they think that Osama bin Laden did, by the way.

It is certainly true that an open society cannot protect itself against every lunatic who thinks he has a cause and a grievance. Necessary precautions must not be allowed to change the nature of this country from what makes it great and strong—its free people whose democratic and enterprising spirit has brought the United States to an apex of power. If Adolf Hitler could not bomb Britain into submission with the Blitz of London [during World War II], which likewise targeted the civilian population, surely the actions of the terrorists yesterday ought only to strengthen American resolve against the evil forces they represent. Americans, bless their hearts, have a way of rising to the occa-

sion. Now the Bush administration has to do the same.

Excerpted from "A Day of Infamy," by Helle Bering, *Washington Times*, September 12, 2001. Copyright © 2001 by Newsworld Communications, Inc. Reprinted with permission of the *Washington Times*.

Wanted: Dead or Alive

Almost immediately, the U.S. government placed the blame for the September 11, 2001, attacks at the feet of Osama bin Laden. At a press conference at the Pentagon in mid-September 2001, President Bush told reporters about the kind of justice he wanted for the reputed terrorist.

Q: *Do you want bin Laden dead?*

THE PRESIDENT: I want justice. There's an old poster out west, as I recall, that said, "Wanted: Dead or Alive."

Q: *Do you see this being long-term? You were saying it's long-term, do you see an end, at all?*

THE PRESIDENT: I think that this is a long-term battle, war. There will be battles. But this is long-term. After all, our mission is not just Osama bin Laden, the al Qaeda organization. Our mission is to battle terrorism and to join with freedom-loving people.

We are putting together a coalition that is a coalition dedicated to declaring to the world we will do what it takes to find the terrorists, to rout them out and to hold them accountable. And the United States is proud to lead the coalition.

Q: *Are you saying you want him dead or alive, sir? Can I interpret—*

Wanted signs of Osama bin Laden have been posted on buildings, subway stations, and bus shelters around New York City.

THE PRESIDENT: I just remember, all I'm doing is remembering when I was a kid I remember that they used to put out there in the Old West, a wanted poster. It said: "Wanted, Dead or Alive." All I want and America wants him brought to justice. That's what we want.

Excerpted from George W. Bush's "Remarks by President to Employees at the Pentagon," September 17, 2001.

 ## A Vote Against U.S. Military Action

Following the attacks of September 11, 2001, President George W. Bush requested that Congress pass a bill that would give him unlimited authority to use military force in response to terrorist attacks. Bush's bill passed both houses of Congress with Representative Barbara Lee of California casting the sole dissenting vote. Below is her statement explaining her vote.

I rise today with a heavy heart, one that is filled with sorrow for the families and loved ones who were killed and injured this week. Only the most foolish or the most callous would not understand the grief that has gripped our people and millions across the world.

This unspeakable attack on the United States has forced me to rely on my moral compass, my conscience, and my God for direction.

September 11 changed the world. Our deepest fears now haunt us. Yet I am convinced that military action will not prevent further acts of international terrorism against the United States.

This resolution will pass although we all know that the President can wage a war even without it. However difficult this vote may be, some of us must urge the use of restraint. Our country is in a state of mourning. Some of us must say, let's step back for a moment and think through the implications of our action today so that it does not spiral out of control.

I have agonized over this vote. But I came to grips with opposing this resolution during the very painful memorial service today. As a member of the clergy so eloquently said, "As we act, let us not become the evil that we deplore."

Excerpted from Representative Barbara Lee's (D-CA) "Statement in Opposition to S.J. Res. 23, Authorizing the Use of Military Force," September 14, 2001.

 ## An Attack on Civilized Values

In the war against terrorism, the United States realized that it needed the entire world's support in order to win the fight. In a speech delivered in October 2001, and excerpted below, Tony Blair, Great Britains prime minister, explains to the House of Commons why Great Britain must support the United States in its war on terrorism.

At 5.30 P.M. British Time yesterday a series of air and cruise missile attacks began on the terrorist camps of Usama Bin Laden and the military installations of the Taliban regime. These were carried out by American and British armed forces with the support of other allies. There were 30 targets: 23 were outside the main cities; 3 were in Kabul and 4 were in the vicinity of other large settlements. In all cases, the utmost care was taken to avoid civilian casualties. British forces were engaged in this action through the use of submarine-launched Tomahawk missiles fired against terrorist training facilities.

British prime minister, Tony Blair, has supported military action against Osama bin Laden's terrorist network.

It is too early to report back fully on the effect of last night's action. However we can say that initial indications are that the coalition operations were successful in achieving their objective of destroying and degrading elements of the Al Qaida terrorist facilities and the Taliban military apparatus that protects them. These operations will continue, and I can tell the House that a second wave of attacks is now under way.

In time, they will be supported by other actions, again carefully targeted on the military network of the enemy.

We took almost four weeks after 11 September to act. I pay tribute to President Bush's statesmanship in having the patience to wait. This was for three reasons. First, we had to establish who was responsible. Once it was clear that the Al Qaida network planned and perpetrated the attacks we then wanted to give the Taliban regime time to decide their own position: would they shield bin Laden or yield him up? It was only fair to give them an ultimatum and time to respond. It is now clear they have chosen to side with terrorism.

But thirdly, we wanted time to make sure that the targets for any action, minimised the possibility of civilian casualties. Our argument is not with the Afghan people. They are victims of the Taliban regime. They live in poverty, repressed viciously, women denied even the most basic human rights and subject to a crude form of theocratic dictatorship that is as cruel as it is arbitrary.

We are doing all we can to limit the effect of our action on ordinary Afghans. I repeat: we will not walk away from them, once the conflict ends, as has happened in the past. We will stand by them and help them to a better, more stable future under a broad-based Government involving all the different ethnic groupings. That is our pledge to the people of Afghanistan. . . .

In the Arab world there has been widespread condemnation of the 11 September atrocities and acceptance of the need to take action against the Al Qaida network.

Of course, Al Qaida and the Taliban regime will be eager to spread false propaganda. Already, their lie machine is putting out false claims about US planes being shot down. There will be much more of this kind of thing. And of course they lie about our motivation. We know their aim. It is to foment [incite] conflict between Islam and the West; it is to present themselves as champions of the Muslim world against the USA. It is to say we are anti-Islam. This is a lie. Let us expose it once and for all. We are in conflict with bin Laden and the Taliban regime because the terrorists killed thousands of innocent people, including hundreds of Muslims and women and children; and because the Taliban regime in return for financial and other support, give them succour [aid].

Forgive me for repeating this, but my visit to Pakistan convinced me these sentiments cannot be repeated too often. To kill in this way is utterly foreign to all teachings of the Koran. To justify it by saying such murder of the innocent is doing the will of God, is to defame the good name of Islam. That is why Muslims the world over have been appalled by this act. This was made clear to me once more at my meeting earlier today with lead-

A compound, belonging to a former Taliban leader, was destroyed by U.S. air strikes in Kandahar.

ers of all the religious faiths in Britain. And for those who doubted bin Laden's wickedness, or his murderous intent, just listen to his television broadcast yesterday. He said: "God Almighty hit the US at its most vulnerable spot. He destroyed its greatest buildings and filled the country with terror. Praise be to God." Sitting next to him, was Ayman al-Zawahiri [a-Zahiri], leader of the Egyptian Islamic Jihad, involved themselves in Al Qaida's attacks on the US Embassies in East Africa in 1998.

I would also remind people of this. When hundreds of thousands of Muslims were subject to ethnic cleansing by the hated Milosevic regime in 1999 in Kosovo, we took military action in Serbia against Milosevic. We weren't acting then against Milosevic because Serbia is an Orthodox Christian country; or in favour of the Kosovars because many are Muslims. We acted against Milosevic because what he was doing—the humanitarian catastrophe he was inflicting on them—was unjust. We helped the Kosovars because they were victims of his injustice.

It is justice too that makes our coalition as important on the humanitarian side as on the military.

We have established an effective coalition to deal with the humanitarian crisis in the region, which of course existed before 11 September.

Our priority has been to re-establish food supply routes into Afghanistan. Some 5,000 tons of food went in during the last fortnight, thanks to the efforts of the UN and other international agencies.

At the UN meeting in Geneva over the weekend, donors pledged $600 million including the UK's own commitment of $55 million.

We will do all we can to help refugees from the Taliban. All we ask them to do is not to stop that help getting through.

We must safeguard our country too. Our first responsibility is the safety of the public. Since 11 September every one of our arrangements has been under scrutiny. We have extensive contingency planning in place in Britain. We are doing all we reasonably can to anticipate the nature of and thwart, any potential reprisal. As yet there is no specific credible threat that we know of against Britain, but we would be foolish to be anything other than highly vigilant, though as the experience of the USA shows it is not an easy task. Contacts between the UK, US and other Governments and agencies are good, and expertise and planning are being shared.

I am aware of the anguish for the families of the aid workers held in Afghanistan, and of the journalist Yvonne Ridley [held by the Taliban]. We hope that the report of her release are correct; but as yet have no official confirmation.

We are in this for the long haul.

Even when Al Qaida is dealt with, the job is not over. The network of international terrorism is not confined to it.

It is essential therefore that we reflect why it is so necessary we stand with the US and other allies in this fight.

It is that this attack was an attack not on the West or the US alone. It was an attack on civilised values everywhere. It was an attempt to change by terror what the terrorists knew they couldn't do by reasoned argument. It was an attempt to substitute terrorist atrocity for deliberative policy; to see the world run by the chaos consequent on terrorist outrage, rather than by disciplined and calm debate.

We in Britain have the most direct interest in defeating such terror. It strikes at the heart of what we believe in. We know that if not stopped, the terrorists will do it again, this time possibly in Britain. We know that it was an attack on economic confidence, trying to destroy the strength of our economies and that eradicating this threat is crucial to global economic confidence. We know the Taliban regime is largely funded by the drugs trade, and that 90 per cent of the heroin on British streets originates in Afghanistan. We know that the refugee crisis, $4\frac{1}{2}$ million on the move even before 11 September, directly impacts on us here.

So this military action we are undertaking is not for a just cause alone, though this cause is just. It is to protect our country, our people, our economy, our way of life. It is not a struggle remote from our everyday concerns. It touches them intimately.

We did not choose this conflict.

We do not lightly go to fight. We are, all of us—the nations involved in this action—peaceful peoples who prefer to live in peace.

But a desire to live in peace should never be interpreted as weakness by those who attack us. If attacked, we will respond; we will defend ourselves; and our very reluctance to use force means that when we do, we do so with complete determination that it shall prevail.

That is why we were there last night in action, and why we will be there again, with our allies. It is why we will continue to act, with steadfast resolve, to see this struggle through to the end and to the victory that would mark the victory not of revenge but of justice over the evil of terrorism.

Excerpted from Tony Blair's "Prime Minister's Statement to the House of Commons," October 8, 2001.

A New Kind of War

In the New York Times *article printed below, U.S. Secretary of Defense, Donald H. Rumsfeld, explains why the U.S.–led war against terrorism is different from any other war the United States has fought and that, despite the differences, he believes the United States will once again be victorious.*

President Bush is rallying the nation for a war against terrorism's attack on our way of life. Some believe the first casualty of any war is the truth. But in this war, the first victory must be to tell the truth. And the truth is, this will be a war like none other our nation has faced. Indeed, it is easier to describe what lies ahead by talking about what it is not rather than what it is.

This war will not be waged by a grand alliance united for the single purpose of defeating an axis of hostile powers. Instead, it will involve floating coalitions of countries, which may change and evolve. Countries will have different roles and contribute in different ways. Some will provide diplomatic support, others financial, still others logistical or military. Some will help us publicly, while others, because of their circumstances, may help us privately and secretly. In this war, the mission will define the coalition—not the other way around.

We understand that countries we consider our friends may help with certain efforts or be silent on others, while other actions we take may depend on the involvement of countries we have considered less than friendly.

In this context, the decision by the United Arab Emirates and Saudi Arabia—friends of the United States—to break ties with the Taliban is an important early success of this campaign, but should not suggest they will be a part of every action we may contemplate.

This war will not necessarily be one in which we pore over military targets and mass forces to seize those targets. Instead, military force will likely be one of many tools we use to stop individuals, groups and countries that engage in terrorism.

Our response may include firing cruise missiles into military targets somewhere in the world; we are just as likely to engage in electronic combat to track and stop investments moving through offshore banking centers. The uniforms of this conflict will be bankers' pinstripes and programmers' grunge just as assuredly as desert camouflage.

This is not a war against an individual, a group, a religion or a country. Rather, our opponent is a global network of terrorist organizations and their state sponsors, committed to denying free people the opportunity to live as they choose. While we may engage militarily against foreign governments that sponsor terrorism, we may also seek to make allies of the people those governments suppress.

Even the vocabulary of this war will be different. When we "invade the enemy's territory," we may well be invading his cyberspace. There may not be as many beachheads stormed as opportunities denied. Forget about "exit strategies"; we're looking at a sustained engagement that carries no deadlines. We have no fixed rules about how to deploy our troops; we'll instead establish guidelines to determine whether military force is the best way to achieve a given objective.

The public may see some dramatic military engagements that produce no apparent victory, or may be unaware of other actions that lead to major victories. "Battles" will be fought by customs officers stopping suspicious persons at our borders and diplomats securing cooperation against money laundering.

But if this is a different kind of war, one thing is unchanged: America remains indomitable. Our victory will come with Americans living their lives day by day, going to work, raising their children and building their dreams as they always have—a free and great people.

Excerpted from "A New Kind of War," by Donald Rumsfeld, *New York Times*, September 27, 2001.

A Widow's Plea for Nonviolence

Amber Amundson's husband, Craig, was killed at the Pentagon on September 11, 2001. Two weeks later, Amundson wrote the following editorial, arguing that her husband would not have wanted the United States to avenge his death with a war.

My husband, Craig Scott Amundson, of the U.S. Army lost his life in the line of duty at the Pentagon on Sept. 11 as the world looked on in horror and disbelief.

Losing my 28-year-old husband and father of our two young children is a terrible and painful experience.

His death is also part of an immense national loss and I am comforted by knowing so many share my grief.

But because I have lost Craig as part of this historic tragedy, my anguish is compounded exponentially by fear that his death will be used to justify new violence against other innocent victims.

I have heard angry rhetoric by some Americans, including many of our nation's leaders, who advise a heavy dose of revenge and punishment. To those leaders, I would like to make clear that my family and I take no comfort in your words of rage. If you choose to respond to this incomprehensible brutality by perpetuating violence against other innocent human beings, you may not do so in the name of justice for my husband. Your words and imminent acts of revenge only amplify our family's suffering, deny us the dignity of remembering our loved one in a way that would have made him proud, and mock his vision of America as a peacemaker in the world community.

Craig enlisted in the Army and was proud to serve his country. He was a patriotic American and a citizen of the world. Craig believed that by working from within the military system he could help to maintain the military focus on peacekeeping and strategic planning—to prevent violence and war. For the last two years Craig drove to his job at the Pentagon with a "visualize world peace" bumper sticker on his car. This was not empty rhetoric or contradictory to him, but part of his dream. He believed his role in the Army could further the cause of peace throughout the world.

Craig would not have wanted a violent response to avenge his death. And I cannot see how good can come out of it. We cannot solve violence with violence. [Indian nationalist leader] Mohandas Gandhi said, "An eye

Government officials survey the damage at "ground zero" where the World Trade Center's twin towers once stood.

for an eye only makes the whole world blind." We will no longer be able to see that we hold the light of liberty if we are blinded by vengeance, anger and fear. I ask our nation's leaders not to take the path that leads to more widespread hatreds—that make my husband's death just one more in an unending spiral of killing.

I call on our national leaders to find the courage to respond to this incomprehensible tragedy by breaking the cycle of violence. I call on them to marshal this great nation's skills and resources to lead a worldwide dialogue on freedom from terror and hate.

I do not know how to begin making a better world: I do believe it must be done, and I believe it is our leaders' responsibility to find a way. I urge them to take up this challenge and respond to our nation's and my personal tragedy with a new beginning that gives us hope for a peaceful global community.

Excerpted from "A Widow's Plea for non-Violence," *Chicago Tribune,* September 25, 2001. Copyright © 2001 by the *Chicago Tribune.* Reprinted with permission.

For Further Reading

Books

Giorgio Baravalle and Cari Modine, eds., *New York September Eleven Two Thousand One.* Milbrook, NY: de.Mo, 2001. This book contains a riveting collection of photographs, personal narratives, poems, and essays by rescue workers, officials, journalists, and others.

Jennifer Bishop, ed., *Through the Eyes of Freedom: A Teen Perspective on September 11, 2001.* Oklahoma City, OK: New Horizons, 2001. This poetry anthology was written mostly by teens in response to the attacks on the United States and the aftermath.

Editors of Andrews McMeel Publishing, ed., with the Poynter Institute, *September 11, 2001.* Kansas City, MO: Andrews McMeel, 2001. The Poynter Institute, a journalism school, compiled 150 front pages from major newspapers throughout the world announcing the news of the terrorist attacks on the United States on September 11.

Editors of Life Magazine, *One Nation: America Remembers September 11, 2001.* Boston, MA: Little, Brown, 2001. The editors have compiled a complete history of the events of September 11, from the building of the World Trade Center, to a minute-by-minute description of the attacks and the heroes who emerged.

Magnum Photographers, with an introduction by David Halberstam, *New York September 11.* New York: Powerhouse Books, 2001. An excellent photographic record of the disaster in New York City on September 11.

Jackie Waldman with Brenda Welchlin and Karen Frost, *America September 11: The Courage to Give: The Triumph of the Human Spirit.* Berkeley, CA: Conari Press, 2001. This book contains a collection of personal stories by firefighters, rescue workers, relatives of the missing, and others.

Periodicals

Karen Breslau, Eleanor Clift, and Evan Thomas, "What Really Happened on Flight 93," *Newsweek,* December 3, 2001.

Richard Brookhiser, "Culture Clash," *National Review,* November 5, 2001.

Angie Cannon, "The 'Other' Tragedy," *U.S. News & World Report,* December 10, 2001.

Noam Chomsky, interviewed by David Barsamian, "The United States Is a Leading Terrorist State," *Monthly Review,* November 2001.

Alexander Cockburn, "Faceless Cowards?" *Nation,* October 1, 2001.

Harvey Cox, "Religion and the War Against Evil," *Nation,* December 24, 2001.

Richard Falk, "A Just Response," *Nation,* October 8, 2001.

Charles Krauthammer, "The Hundred Days: Fifty Years of World War. Ten Years of Slumber. And Now, America Awakes," *Time,* December 31, 2001.

Miriam Ching Louie, "The 9/11 Disappeareds," *Nation,* December 3, 2001.

Lance Morrow, "The Case for Rage and Retribution," *Time,* September 14, 2001.

National Review, "Special Section: At War," October 1, 2001.

New Republic, "It Happened Here," September 24, 2001.

Amanda Ripley, "Facing the End," *Time,* September 24, 2001.

Hazem Saghiyeh, "It's Not All America's Fault," *Time,* October 15, 2001.

Suzanne Smalley et al., "The Kids Who Saw It All," *Newsweek,* October 15, 2001.

Evan Thomas, "The Day that Changed America," *Newsweek,* December 31, 2001.

David Whitman, "Timeline of Horror," *U.S. News & World Report,* September 14, 2001.

Fareed Zakaria, "The Politics of Rage: Why Do They Hate Us?" *Newsweek,* October 15, 2001.

Websites

The September 11 Web Archive (http://September11.archive.org). Probably the most comprehensive website covering the attacks of September 11, 2001. This website was commissioned by the Library of Congress to preserve websites established following the events of September 11, 2001, and includes government, military, charitable organizations, national and international news sites.

Index

Picture Credits

Cover: © Carmen Taylor/AP Wide World
   Photo
© AFP/CORBIS, 20, 42, 44, 47, 55, 67, 73,
   83
© Bettmann/CORBIS, 63
© Paul Colangelo/CORBIS, 16

© Mitchell Gerber/CORBIS, 27
© Eye Ubiquitous/CORBIS, 39
Chris Jouan, 19
© Wally McNamee/CORBIS, 65
© ReutersNewMedia/CORBIS, 11, 12, 14,
   25, 29, 32, 35, 50, 53, 65, 80, 81, 87

About the Author

Tamara L. Roleff is a freelance writer and former senior editor for Greenhaven Press. She has a degree in English from Iowa State University and worked as a newspaper reporter and editor before editing books for Greenhaven Press. She has lived and traveled all over the world, but San Diego will always be her home.